The Ultimate Lean and Green Cookbook for Beginners

1000 Days Easy and Delicious Recipes to Help You Manage Figure and Keep Healthy by Harnessing the Power of "Fueling Hacks Meals"

Blanche Hogan

Table of Contents

INTRODUCTION 5

    What is the Lean and Green Diet? 5

    How to Follow the Diet 6

    Potential Benefits of the Lean and Green Diet 6

    How Easy is the Lean and Green Diet to Follow? 7

    What to Eat and Avoid On the Lean and Green Diet 7

FUELINGS RECIPE HACKS 9

    Buffalo Cauliflower Wings 9

    Mashed Potato and Grilled Cheese Waffles 10

    Red Velvet Cream Pies 11

    Greek Yogurt Sticks 12

    Pecan and Sweet Potato Muffins 13

    Sweet Potato and Goat's Cheese Quiche 14

    Chocolate Berry Parfait 15

    Peanut Butter Energy Bites 16

    Guacamole with Zesty Tortilla Chips 17

    Honey Chicken Nuggets with Mustard Dip 18

    Oatmeal Breakfast Cookies 19

    Cheesy Savory Waffles 20

    Cheesy Mashed Potatoes with Spinach 21

    Honey Cinnamon Baked Oatmeal 22

    Taco Salad 23

    Crunchy Caramel Parfait 24

    Yogurt Berry Bagel with Cream Cheese 25

    Lemon Bites 26

    Tropical Smoothie Bowl 27

    Chocolate Coconut Cream Pie 28

    Brownie Pies with Peanut Butter 29

    Pumpkin Chocolate Cheesecake 30

    Mocha Cherry Pops 31

    Gingerbread Trifle 32

    Coconut Colada Shake 33

    Shrimp Cobb Salad 34

    Chocolaty Peanut Butter Donuts 35

    Cinnamon Bun Brownies 36

    Skinny Peppermint Mocha 37

    Yogurt Donut with Cream Cheese 38

LEAN AND GREEN RECIPES 39

    Salmon Burger with Cucumber Salad 39

    Vegetable Tofu Bowl with Eggs 40

    Chicken Caesar Salad 41

    Mediterranean Chicken and Vegetables 42

    Minestrone Soup 43

    Shredded Beef Stew 44

    Chicken Soy Chorizo Paella 45

    Chicken Meatballs and Napa Cabbage in Ginger Broth 46

    Chicken Kohlrabi Noodles Soup 47

    Parmesan Meatballs with Collard Greens 48

    Spaghetti Squash Lasagna 49

Zucchini Lasagna 50

Shepherd's Pie with Mashed Cauliflower 51

Broccoli Cheddar Breakfast Bake 52

Blackened Shrimp Lettuce Wraps 53

Cheeseburger Soup 54

Mexican Bell Pepper Casserole 55

Zucchini Pad Thai Noodles 56

Maple Turkey Patties with Spaghetti Squash Hash Brown 57

Egg Muffins with Kale, Tomatoes, and Goat's Cheese 59

Spaghetti Squash Bolognese 60

Pepper Jack and Spinach Breakfast Burrito ... 61

Shrimp Fried Cauliflower Rice 62

Buffalo Chicken Dip and Veggie Chips 63

Tuna Niçoise Salad 64

Crabmeat and Asparagus Frittata 65

Savory Cilantro Salmon 66

Stuffed Eggplant with Shrimp and Cauliflower Rice 67

Chilies Rellenos Omelet 68

Huevos Rancheros 69

Bell Pepper Eggs 70

Cumin Tacos De Bistec 71

Beef Stew over Mashed Cauliflower 72

Cincinnati Chili 73

Cloud Bread 74

Cauliflower Tortillas 75

4-Ingredients Skinny Queso 76

Pepper Nachos 77

Chicken with Tomato Braised Cauliflower 78

Vegetable and Turkey Pizza 79

Turkey Chili 80

Chicken Cacciatore 81

Baked Pork Chops with Sautéed Chard and Mushrooms 82

Ropa Vieja 83

Lemony Garlicky Chicken with Asparagus 84

Chicken Pho 85

Arroz Con Pollo 86

Tropical Chicken Medley 87

Shrimp Scampi 88

Crabmeat Burger with Salad 89

LEAN AND GREEN MEAL PLAN 5 & 1 90

Week 1 90

Week 2 91

Week 3 92

Week 4 93

LEAN AND GREEN MEAL PLAN 4 & 2 & 1 95

Week 1 95

Week 2 96

Week 3 98

Week 4 99

CONCLUSION 101

INTRODUCTION

What is the Lean and Green Diet?

The Lean and Green diet is a low-calorie, reduced-carb program that combines ready-made or packaged foods, snacks, and drinks with homemade mini-meals ("fuelings") and meals. The meal plans are designed to stimulate weight loss, and by following them, you can shed pounds while eating healthily. You will find your energy boosted, and you won't feel starved.

The Lean and Green diet comprises ingredients that are low in carbs but high in protein and probiotics cultures. Plus, each fueling includes friendly bacteria to boost your gut health. These mini-meals include bars, cookies, shakes, puddings, cereals, soups, pasta dishes, and more. Fuelings are considered to be lower in carbs and sugar than conventional versions of the same foods. They contain sugar substitutes and small portion sizes.

The Lean and Green Diet

The Lean and Green diet includes two weight loss programs and one weight maintenance plan:

- **Optimal Weight 5 & 1 Plan.** This beginner's plan includes five fuelings and one balanced Lean and Green meal each day.

- **Optimal Weight 4 & 2 & 1 Plan.** This plan is designed for those who need more calories and flexibility in their food choices. It entails four fuelings, two Lean and Green meals, and one snack per day.
- **Optimal Health 3 & 3 Plan.** This plan is designed for weight maintenance. It has three fuelings and three balanced Lean and Green meals per day.

Most Lean and Green dieters opt for the Optimal Weight 5 & 1 Plan, comprising five fuelings a day. You can choose from more than 50 options, including shakes, bars, soups, cookies, and pudding, all of which contain high-quality protein. Your sixth daily meal, which you can have whenever you desire, contains cooked lean protein, three servings of non-starchy vegetables, and healthy fats.

People looking for a slightly more flexible and higher-calorie diet can go for the Optimal Weight 4 & 2 & 1 Plan. This meal plan includes four fuelings, two Lean and Green meals, and one healthy snack, such as fruit or a baked potato, a day.

How to Follow the Diet

Whichever plan you choose, you have to start by setting weight loss goals and becoming familiar with the program.

- **Initial Steps**

For weight loss, the Optimal Weight 5 & 1 Plan is best. This meal plan sets out to provide 800 to 1,000 calories per day, helping you drop 11.9 pounds over 12 weeks.

- **Maintenance Phase**

When you reach your preferred weight, you go into a six-week transition phase. You will gradually increase your calorie intake to no more than 1,550 calories per day. This phase involves adding in a variety of foods, including whole grains, fruits, and low-fat dairy.

After six weeks, you're meant to move onto the Optimal Health 3 & 3 Plan, which includes three Lean and Green meals and three fuelings daily, plus continued coaching.

Potential Benefits of the Lean and Green Diet

This diet boosts weight loss and improves health, and also has the following additional benefits.

- **Easy to follow**

As the diet regularly relies on prepackaged fuelings, you're only accountable for cooking one meal per day on the 5 & 1 Plan. Each plan comes with meal logs, and sample meal plans to follow.

While you're encouraged to cook one to three Lean and Green meals per day (depending on the plan you choose), they're simple and easy to make. The program includes precise recipes and a list of food options.

In addition, those who aren't interested in cooking can buy pre-packaged meals called "Flavors of Home" to replace the Lean and Green meals.

- **May improve blood pressure**

The Lean and Green program helps improve blood pressure through weight loss and limited sodium intake.

The Lean and Green meal plans are designed to provide less than 2,300 mg of sodium per day. Higher sodium intake can increase the risk of high blood pressure and heart disease in salt-sensitive individuals. This program's recipes provide balanced salt intake, which is helpful for heart health and blood pressure.

- **Offers ongoing support**

Health coaches are available throughout the weight loss and maintenance programs.

How Easy is the Lean and Green Diet to Follow?

Following the Lean and Green diet is simple. You have more than 50 fueling options on the program. You get to eat every couple of hours and don't have to track your food intake. There is no need to count carbs, points, or calories, as these are all included in the meal plans for you.

Exercise and the Lean and Green diet

A Lean and Green diet emphasizes 30 minutes of moderate-intensity exercise a day. Choose something you enjoy and can easily incorporate into your daily routine, like walking. Start slowly, and over time you can gradually increase the minutes you spend exercising.

What to Eat and Avoid On the Lean and Green Diet

Foods that are allowed

The foods that you can eat in your daily meal include:

- **Meat:** chicken, turkey, lean beef, lamb, pork chop or tenderloin, ground meat (at least 90% lean)
- **Fish and shellfish:** halibut, trout, salmon, tuna, lobster, crab, shrimp, scallops
- **Eggs:** whole eggs, egg whites, Egg Beaters
- **Soy products:** only tofu
- **Oils:** canola, flaxseed, walnut, and olive oil
- **Healthy fats:** low-carb salad dressings, olives, reduced-fat margarine, almonds, walnuts, pistachios, avocado
- **Low-carb vegetables:** collard greens, spinach, celery, cucumbers, mushrooms, cabbage, cauliflower, eggplant, zucchini, broccoli, peppers, spaghetti squash
- **Sugar-free snacks:** popsicles, gelatin, gum, mints
- **Sugar-free beverages:** water, unsweetened almond milk, tea, coffee

- **Condiments and seasonings:** dried herbs, spices, salt, lemon juice, lime juice, yellow mustard, soy sauce, salsa, sugar-free syrup, zero-calorie sweeteners, only half a teaspoon of ketchup, cocktail sauce, or barbecue sauce

Foods to avoid

Most carb-containing foods and beverages are banned while on the 5 & 1 Plan. Certain fats are also limited, as are all fried foods:

- **Fried foods:** meats, fish, shellfish, vegetables, pastries, donuts
- **Refined grains:** pasta, biscuits, pancakes, flour tortillas, crackers, white rice, cookies, cakes, pastries
- **Certain fats:** butter, coconut oil, solid shortening
- **Whole fat dairy:** milk, cheese, yogurt
- **Alcohol:** all varieties
- **Sugar-sweetened beverages:** soda, fruit juice, sports drinks, energy drinks, sweet tea

The following foods are off-limits (even on the 5 & 1 Plan) but can be added back during the six-week transition phase. They are also allowed on the 3 & 3 Plan:

- **Fruit:** all fresh fruit
- **Low-fat or fat-free dairy:** yogurt, milk, cheese
- **Whole grains:** whole grain bread, high fiber breakfast cereal, brown rice, whole-wheat pasta
- **Legumes:** peas, lentils, beans, soybeans
- **Starchy vegetables:** sweet potatoes, white potatoes, corn, peas

FUELINGS RECIPE HACKS

Buffalo Cauliflower Wings

Prep Time: 10 minutes
Cook Time: 25 minutes
Serves: 2

Ingredients:
- 2 sachets Buttermilk Cheddar Herb Biscuit, crumbled
- ½ cup water
- 3 cups cauliflower florets
- Cooking spray
- ¼ cup hot Buffalo sauce
- ½ tablespoon butter, melted
- ¼ cup low-fat plain Greek yogurt
- 1 teaspoon dry ranch dressing mix

Preparation:
1. Preheat the oven to 400°F. Lightly grease a lined baking sheet.
2. Mix together the biscuits and water in a bowl. Add the cauliflower and toss well until the florets are thoroughly and evenly coated.
3. Place the coated florets on the baking sheet and bake for 20 minutes.
4. Meanwhile, in a medium bowl, mix the hot Buffalo sauce and butter.
5. Add the baked cauliflower and toss in the sauce well. Place the mixture back onto the baking sheet and bake for 5 more minutes.
6. In another bowl, combine the yogurt and ranch dressing mix for dipping.

Serving Suggestion: Serve Buffalo cauliflower wings with the ranch dressing mixture.

Variation Tip: Add chopped chives for garnishing.

Nutritional Information Per Serving:
Calories 116 | Carbohydrates 13g | Protein 2g | Fat 5g | Sodium 1577mg | Fiber 1g

Mashed Potato and Grilled Cheese Waffles

Prep Time: 5 minutes
Cook Time: 10 minutes
Serves: 2

Ingredients:

- 2 sachets Essential Roasted Garlic Creamy Smashed Potatoes
- 1 cup water
- 1 cup low-fat cheese (cheddar, mozzarella)

Preparation:

1. In a microwave-safe, medium bowl, thoroughly combine the smashed potatoes mix and water. Microwave on high for 30 seconds and stir well.
2. Pour this mixture onto a hot, lightly greased waffle iron and cook for about 10 minutes.
3. Sprinkle cheese on one-half of the waffles and fold the other half. Close the waffle iron and cook the waffles for another 2 to 3 minutes until done or the cheese has melted.

Serving Suggestion: Serve with dill garnishing or enjoy as it is.

Variation Tip: Use chopped dill for garnish.

Nutritional Information Per Serving:

Calories 150 | Carbohydrates 24g | Protein 4g | Fat 5g | Sodium 680mg| Fiber 1g

Red Velvet Cream Pies

Prep Time: 10 minutes
Cook Time: 15 minutes
Serves: 4

Ingredients:
- 2 sachets Essential Golden Chip Pancakes mix
- 2 sachets Essential Chewy Chocolate Chip Cookie mix
- ½ tablespoon unsweetened cocoa powder
- ½ teaspoon baking powder
- ½ cup unsweetened almond milk
- 6 tablespoons liquid egg substitute
- 1 teaspoon apple cider vinegar
- Cooking spray
- ½ cup low-fat cream cheese
- 1-2 packets zero calories sugar substitute

Preparation:

1. Preheat the oven to 350°F.
2. Combine the pancake mix, chocolate chip cookies mix, cocoa powder, and baking powder in a bowl.
3. Add the milk, eggs, and apple cider vinegar and mix until it has a batter-like consistency.
4. Divide the batter among eight muffins tins and bake for 15 to 20 minutes.
5. Mix the cream cheese and sugar substitute until they are well combined.
6. Once the pies have cooled, slice each in half horizontally, spread the cream filling, and sandwich the halves back together.

Serving Suggestion: Serve the pies topped with whipped cream.

Variation Tip: Add red color to the batter for a red velvet pie.

Nutritional Information Per Serving:
Calories 472 | Carbohydrates 82g | Protein 4.4g | Fat 14.5g | Sodium 505mg| Fiber 1.7g

Greek Yogurt Sticks

Prep Time: 2 minutes
Cook Time: 8 minutes
Serves: 2

Ingredients:

- 12 ounces plain low-fat Greek yogurt
- 1-2 packets zero-calorie sugar substitute
- 1 sachet Essential Red Berry Crunchy O's Cereal, crushed

Preparation:

1. In a medium-sized bowl, combine the Greek yogurt and sugar substitute.
2. Line an 8x8 inch baking dish with non-stick foil. Spread the Greek yogurt/sugar mix in an even layer onto the foil.
3. Sprinkle the crushed cereal on top of the mix.
4. Freeze for 4 to 5 hours or overnight until the bar is hard.

Serving Suggestion: Break the bar into smaller pieces with a sharp knife. Store leftovers in freezer-safe bags or containers in the freezer.

Variation Tip: Add chopped nuts for extra crunch.

Nutritional Information Per Serving:

Calories 100 | Carbohydrates 0g | Protein 6g | Fat 9g | Sodium 120mg| Fiber 0g

Pecan and Sweet Potato Muffins

Prep Time: 10 minutes
Cook Time: 20 minutes
Serves: 4

Ingredients:

- 2 sachets Select Honey Sweet Potatoes
- 1 cup cold water
- 2 sachets Essential Spiced Gingerbread
- 6 tablespoons liquid egg substitute
- ¼ cup unsweetened vanilla almond milk
- ½ teaspoon pumpkin pie spice
- ½ teaspoon vanilla extract
- ½ teaspoon baking powder
- Cooking spray
- 1⅓ cups pecans, chopped

Preparation:

1. Preheat the oven to 350°F.
2. Prepare the potatoes according to the directions. Let the mix cool slightly.
3. In a medium-sized bowl, combine the cooked potatoes and the remaining ingredients (except for the pecans).
4. Divide the mixture amongst eight slots on a lightly-greased standard-sized muffin pan. Sprinkle the tops with chopped pecans. Bake for 20 minutes.

Serving Suggestion: Serve with hot tea.

Variation Tip: Add chopped almonds instead of pecans.

Nutritional Information Per Serving:
Calories 472 | Carbohydrates 30.6g | Protein 2.9g | Fat 9.8g | Sodium 205mg| Fiber 1.5g

Sweet Potato and Goat's Cheese Quiche

Prep Time: 15 minutes.
Cook Time: 30 minutes.
Serves: 4

Ingredients:

- 4 sachets Select Honey Sweet Potatoes
- 1 cup unsweetened almond milk
- 4 eggs
- ⅔ cup part-skim ricotta cheese
- 1 ounce crumbled goat's cheese
- ¼ cup yellow onion, diced
- 1 tablespoon fresh rosemary, chopped
- ⅛ teaspoon nutmeg
- Cooking spray

Preparation:

1. Preheat the oven to 375°F.
2. In a large, microwave-safe bowl, stir together the potatoes mix and the milk until well combined.
3. Microwave on high for 1½ minutes. When done, stir, and let the mixture sit until thickened and cooled.
4. Add the remaining ingredients, and mix until well combined.
5. Divide the mixture evenly among 12 slots of a standard-sized, lightly-greased muffin tin.
6. Baked for 25 to 30 minutes, until the mixture is set and the edges are brown.

Serving Suggestion: Serve the quiche topped with rosemary.

Variation Tip: Add dill for freshness.

Nutritional Information Per Serving:

Calories 403 | Carbohydrates 47g | Protein 15g | Fat 17g | Sodium 351mg| Fiber 7g

Chocolate Berry Parfait

Prep Time: 2 minutes
Cook Time: 3 minutes
Serves: 2

Ingredients:

- 1½ cups plain, non-fat Greek yogurt
- ¼ cup strawberry-flavored light cream cheese
- 1 tablespoon unsweetened cocoa powder
- 1-2 packets zero-calorie sugar substitute
- 1 Select Chocolate Cherry Ganache Bar
- ⅔ ounce almonds, sliced

Preparation:

1. Place all the ingredients in a blender. Blend on high until the desired consistency is reached.

Serving Suggestion: Serve chilled.

Variation Tip: Sprinkle almonds on top for crunch.

Nutritional Information Per Serving:
Calories 195 | Carbohydrates 42g | Protein 4g | Fat 18g | Sodium 205mg| Fiber 5g

Peanut Butter Energy Bites

Prep Time: 2 minutes
Cook Time: 3 minutes
Serves: 1

Ingredients:

- 1 Essential Creamy Double Peanut Butter Crisp Bar
- 2 tablespoons powdered peanut butter
- 1 tablespoon water

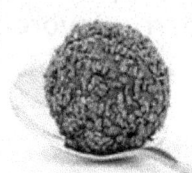

Preparation:

1. Mix the powdered peanut butter and water in a small bowl to form a smooth paste.
2. Place the peanut butter bar on a microwave-safe plate and microwave for 15 seconds or until soft.
3. Combine the warm pieces of the bar with the peanut butter to form a dough.
4. Use a cookie scoop or your fingers to form four bite-sized balls. Refrigerate until ready to serve.

Serving Suggestion: Serve as chilled energy bars.

Variation Tip: Add fresh nuts and unsweetened maple syrup.

Nutritional Information Per Serving:

Calories 189| Carbohydrates 17.5g | Protein 5.4g | Fat 11.8g | Sodium 65.3mg| Fiber 2.9g

Guacamole with Zesty Tortilla Chips

Prep Time: 10 minutes
Cook Time: 10 minutes
Serves: 2

Ingredients:

Chips

- 2 packets Essential Hearty Red Bean & Vegetable Chili
- ¼ cup water
- Cooking spray

Guacamole

- 3 ounces avocado, peeled, pitted, and mashed
- 1 tablespoon pico de gallo
- ½ teaspoon lemon or lime juice
- ⅛ teaspoon salt

Preparation:

1. Preheat the oven to 350°F.
2. Empty the contents of the chili mix packets into a food processor. Pulverize into a fine powder.
3. Transfer the powder into a small mixing bowl. Add water, and whisk until smooth and a dough-like consistency.
4. Place the mixture onto a piece of lightly greased parchment paper. Use your fingers to press the dough into a ¼-inch thick circle. Use a pizza cutter to cut tortilla-shaped pieces.
5. Place the parchment paper with the tortilla-like pieces onto a baking sheet. Bake for 10 minutes, flip, and bake an additional 10 to 15 minutes or until the chips are crispy.
6. Meanwhile, prepare the guacamole. Place the mashed avocado in a small mixing bowl, stir in the remaining ingredients, and refrigerate until ready to serve.

Serving Suggestion: Serve chilled.

Variation Tip: Alternatively, you can eat tortilla chips made from cauliflower with this guacamole.

Nutritional Information Per Serving:
Calories 130 | Carbohydrates 16g | Protein 2g | Fat 7g | Sodium 140mg| Fiber 1g

Honey Chicken Nuggets with Mustard Dip

Prep Time: 10 minutes
Cook Time: 15 minutes
Serves: 2

Ingredients:

- 12 ounces boneless, skinless chicken breast, cubed
- 1 egg, beaten
- 2 sachets Essential Honey Mustard & Onion Sticks, crumbled
- ¼ cup plain low-fat Greek yogurt
- 2 teaspoons spicy brown mustard
- ¼ teaspoon garlic powder
- Cooking spray

Preparation:

1. Preheat the oven to 400°F.
2. Place the egg and crumbled mustard and onion sticks into two separate small, shallow bowls.
3. Dip each chicken piece into the egg, and then roll in the crumbs until completely coated.
4. Place the coated chicken pieces onto a lightly greased, foil-lined baking sheet. Lightly spray the tops with cooking spray.
5. Bake until the coating turns golden and the internal temperature of the chicken pieces reaches 165°F (about 18 to 20 minutes), flipping halfway through.
6. Meanwhile, combine the Greek yogurt, mustard, and garlic powder in a small bowl.

Serving Suggestion: Serve the nuggets with the yogurt dip.

Variation Tip: Add chili flakes for spice.

Nutritional Information Per Serving:

Calories 211 | Carbohydrates 13.6g | Protein 21.9g | Fat 7.7g | Sodium 5.7mg| Fiber 1.4g

Oatmeal Breakfast Cookies

Prep Time: 10 minutes
Cook Time: 25 minutes
Serves: 2

Ingredients:

- 1 sachet Essential Old-Fashioned Maple & Brown Sugar Oatmeal
- 1 Essential Raisin Oat Cinnamon Crisp Bar
- ⅛ teaspoon cinnamon
- 1 packet Stevia
- ⅓ cup water
- ⅛ teaspoon baking powder
- ½ teaspoon vanilla
- 2 tablespoons PB2

Preparation:

1. Preheat the oven to 350°F.
2. Microwave the raisin bar for 15 seconds until slightly melted.
3. Mix the bar with all the other ingredients and let sit for 5 minutes.
4. Line a cookie sheet with parchment paper or spray with cooking spray.
5. Drop spoonfuls of the mixture onto the sheet to make four cookies. Bake for 12-15 minutes.

Serving Suggestion: Serve warm with cold almond milk.

Variation Tip: Add fresh raisins to the mixture for chewiness.

Nutritional Information Per Serving:

Calories 123 | Carbohydrates 24.7g | Protein 3.9g | Fat 1.5g | Sodium 5.7mg| Fiber 2.6g

Cheesy Savory Waffles

Prep Time: 5 minutes
Cook Time: 10 minutes
Serves: 4

Ingredients:

- 4 packets Essential Roasted Garlic Creamy Smashed Potatoes
- ½ cup unsweetened almond or cashew milk
- ½ cup reduced-fat cheddar cheese, shredded
- ½ cup liquid egg substitute
- 2 slices turkey bacon, cooked
- ¼ cup scallions, chopped
- Cooking spray

Preparation:

1. Mix the contents of the potato-mix packets, milk, cheese, and egg substitute in a medium-sized bowl until well combined.
2. Fold in the remaining ingredients.
3. Pour the mixture into a hot, lightly greased waffle iron. Close the lid and bake for 5 to 7 minutes, until golden brown. Carefully remove the waffle and serve.

Serving Suggestion: Serve hot.

Variation Tip: Add some low-fat Greek yogurt as a topping.

Nutritional Information Per Serving:

Calories 115.4 | Carbohydrates 13.6g | Protein 6.0g | Fat 4.3g | Sodium 356.8mg | Fiber 0.5g

Cheesy Mashed Potatoes with Spinach

Prep Time: 10 minutes
Cook Time: 25 minutes
Serves: 1

Ingredients:

- 1 sachet Essential Roasted Garlic Creamy Smashed Potatoes
- 1 cup baby spinach
- 1 teaspoon water
- ½ cup reduced-fat mozzarella cheese, shredded
- 1 tablespoon parmesan cheese, grated

Preparation:

1. Prepare the potatoes as per the box instructions.
2. Steam the spinach with water in the microwave for 1 minute or until wilted.
3. Combine the cooked potatoes, spinach, mozzarella, and parmesan cheese.

Serving Suggestion: Serve hot.

Variation Tip: Add chopped chive to the mix for color.

Nutritional Information Per Serving:

Calories 275.2 | Carbohydrates 48.1g | Protein 6.5g | Fat 7g | Sodium 346.5mg| Fiber 6.1g

Honey Cinnamon Baked Oatmeal

Prep Time: 10 minutes.
Cook Time: 25 minutes.
Serves: 4

Ingredients:

- 4 sachets Essential Cinnamon and Honey Hot Cereal
- ½ teaspoon baking powder
- 3 tablespoons liquid egg substitute
- 1 cup almond milk
- ¼ teaspoon cinnamon
- Cooking spray

Preparation:

1. Preheat the oven to 350°F.
2. In a large bowl, combine the cereal and baking powder.
3. Add the liquid egg white and almond milk; stir until the milk is fully absorbed.
4. Divide the mixture evenly between four lightly-greased mason jars, leaving about half an inch at the top. Sprinkle the tops with cinnamon.
5. Bake for 20 to 25 minutes on a small baking sheet, until slightly firm and golden on top. Allow the mixture to cool completely.

Serving Suggestion: Serve topped with cream cheese.

Variation Tip: Add pecan and walnuts for crunch.

Nutritional Information Per Serving:

Calories 214.7 | Carbohydrates 39.2g | Protein 5.5g | Fat 5.4g | Sodium 28.5mg| Fiber 4.6g

Taco Salad

Prep Time: 5 minutes
Cook Time: 7 minutes
Serves: 2

Ingredients:

- 4 ounces lean ground beef
- ½ teaspoon taco seasoning mix
- ⅓ cup tomatoes, chopped
- 1¾ cup romaine lettuce, shredded
- 1 packet tortilla taco chips

Preparation:

1. In a medium-sized skillet, brown the lean ground beef. Drain the meat and return to the skillet.
2. Stir in the taco seasoning and heat for approximately 2 to 3 minutes. Set aside and let cool.
3. Shred the lettuce and add the chopped tomatoes to the bowl. Mix in the seasoned ground beef.
4. Top the beef salad with the taco chips.

Serving Suggestion: Serve the salad topped with shredded low-fat cheese.

Variation Tip: Add chili flakes to the beef for spiciness.

Nutritional Information Per Serving:

Calories 321.5 | Carbohydrates 25.5g | Protein 17.8g | Fat 16.5g | Sodium 404.9mg| Fiber 5.7g

Crunchy Caramel Parfait

Prep Time: 2 minutes
Cook Time: 3 minutes
Serves: 2

Ingredients:

- 6 ounces plain low-fat Greek yogurt
- ¼ teaspoon vanilla extract
- ½ packet Stevia
- 1 sachet Puffed Sweet & Salty Snacks
- 2 tablespoons light pressurized whipped topping
- 1 tablespoon sugar-free caramel syrup

Preparation:

1. Combine the yogurt and vanilla extract.
2. Break up the puffed snacks into small pieces.
3. Top the yogurt with the whipped topping and the puffed snacks pieces.

Serving Suggestion: Serve the parfait drizzled with syrup.

Variation Tip: Add chopped nuts.

Nutritional Information Per Serving:

Calories 442 | Carbohydrates 58g | Protein 9g | Fat 22g | Sodium 352mg | Fiber 5g

Yogurt Berry Bagel with Cream Cheese

Prep Time: 10 minutes
Cook Time: 10 minutes
Serves: 2

Ingredients:

- 1 sachet Essential Yogurt Berry Blast Smoothie
- ½ cup unsweetened original almond milk
- 2 tablespoons liquid egg substitute
- ½ teaspoon baking powder
- 1 ounce light cream cheese

Preparation:

1. Preheat the oven to 350°F.
2. In a medium-sized bowl, combine the smoothie mix, milk, egg substitute, and baking powder.
3. Divide the mixture among four lightly-greased slots of a donut pan.
4. Bake until the mixture is set, about 12 to 15 minutes.
5. Let cool slightly before serving with cream cheese.

Serving Suggestion: Serve the bagel warm.

Variation Tip: Add ham and vegetables.

Nutritional Information per Serving:
Calories 263| Carbohydrates 46.4g | Protein 8.9g | Fat 4.3g | Sodium 412mg| Fiber 2.3g

Lemon Bites

Prep Time: 5 minutes
Cook Time: 10 minutes
Serves: 2

Ingredients:

- 2 Essential Zesty Lemon Crisp Bars
- 1½ cups low-fat plain Greek yogurt
- 1 (0.3 ounces) sachet sugar-free lemon gelatin
- ½ teaspoon lime zest

Preparation:

1. Line a muffin tin with six cupcake liners.
2. Break each lemon bar into thirds and place in a microwave-safe bowl. Microwave for 10 to 15 seconds.
3. Press the mix into six cupcake liners to form a thin crust.
4. In a microwave-safe bowl, mix the yogurt and gelatin powder. Microwave on high for 2 minutes, stirring after each minute.
5. Pour ¼ cup of the yogurt mixture on top of each crust.
6. Allow the mixture to chill for at least 1 hour. Garnish with lime zest if desired.

Serving Suggestion: Serve chilled topped with lemon zest.

Variation Tip: Add cream cheese for extra cheesiness.

Nutritional Information Per Serving:
Calories 130| Carbohydrates 19g | Protein 1g | Fat 5g | Sodium 95mg| Fiber 0g

Tropical Smoothie Bowl

Prep Time: 2 minutes
Cook Time: 3 minutes
Serves: 1

Ingredients:

- 1 sachet Essential Tropical Fruit Smoothie
- ½ cup unsweetened, original coconut milk
- ½ cup ice
- ½ ounce macadamias or cashews, chopped
- 1 tablespoon unsweetened coconut, shredded
- ½ tablespoon chia seeds
- ½ teaspoon lime zest

Preparation:

1. Add the smoothie mix, milk, and ice to a blender and blend until smooth.
2. Pour the smoothie mixture into a small, shallow bowl.
3. Top with the remaining ingredients, and serve.

Serving Suggestion: Serve chilled.

Variation Tip: Add almond essence or chopped almonds for flavor.

Nutritional Information Per Serving:
Calories 134 | Carbohydrates 17g | Protein 7g | Fat 5.5g | Sodium 25mg | Fiber 2g

Chocolate Coconut Cream Pie

Prep Time: 10 minutes
Cook Time: 30 minutes
Serves: 2

Ingredients:

- 1 Essential Chocolate Fudge Crisp Bar
- 1 serving Essential Chocolate Fudge Pudding
- Cooking spray
- ½ cup unsweetened, original coconut milk
- 2 tablespoons pressurized whipped topping
- 1½ unsweetened coconut, shredded

Preparation:

1. Place the bar on a small, microwave-safe plate and microwave for 15 to 20 seconds.
2. Press the microwaved bar into the bottom of a small, lightly-greased ramekin.
3. In a small bowl, combine the pudding and milk.
4. Pour the mixture over the top of the bar in the ramekin. Refrigerate until set, about 30 minutes.
5. Top with the whipped topping and sprinkle with coconut flakes before serving.

Serving Suggestion: Top with whipped topping and sprinkle with coconut flakes before serving.

Variation Tip: To toast the shredded coconut, spread the flakes onto a baking sheet in an even layer. Bake at 325°F for 5 to 7 minutes, until lightly browned.

Nutritional Information Per Serving:

Calories 320 | Carbohydrates 46g | Protein 4g | Fat 14g | Sodium 320mg | Fiber 1g

Brownie Pies with Peanut Butter

Prep Time: 10 minutes
Cook Time: 15 minutes
Serves: 2 (12 pies per serving)

Ingredients:

- 2 sachets Essential Decadent Double Chocolate Brownie
- ¼ teaspoon baking powder
- 3 tablespoons liquid egg substitute
- 6 tablespoons unsweetened almond milk, divided
- 1 teaspoon vegetable oil
- ¼ cup powder peanut butter
- Cooking spray

Preparation:

1. Preheat the oven to 350°F.
2. In a medium-sized bowl, combine the brownie mixture, baking powder, egg substitute, ¼ cup milk, oil. Mix until you achieve a batter-like consistency.
3. Divide the batter evenly among four slots of a lightly-greased muffin tin. Bake until a toothpick inserted in the center of each pie comes out clean, about 18 to 20 minutes.
4. Meanwhile, combine the powdered peanut butter and remaining milk.

Serving Suggestion: Once cooled, slice each muffin in half horizontally. Spread 1 tablespoon of peanut butter filling onto the bottom half of each muffin and top with the remaining muffin halves. Enjoy!

Variation Tip: Add chopped nuts for crunch.

Nutritional Information Per Serving:
Calories 340 | Carbohydrates 37g | Protein 5g | Fat 21g | Sodium 140mg| Fiber 3g

Pumpkin Chocolate Cheesecake

Prep Time: 5 minutes
Cook Time: 55 minutes
Serves: 2

Ingredients:

- 2 sachets Essential Decadent Double Chocolate Brownie
- ½ tablespoon unsalted butter, melted
- 2 tablespoons cold water
- Cooking spray
- 1 cup plain non-fat Greek yogurt
- 3 tablespoons pumpkin puree
- 1 large egg
- 2 packets Stevia
- ½ teaspoon pumpkin pie spice
- ½ teaspoon vanilla extract
- 1 pinch Salt

Preparation:

1. Preheat the oven to 350°F.
2. In a small bowl, combine the brownie mix with the butter and water.
3. Divide the brownie mixture evenly among two lightly-greased mini pans, pressing it into the bottom of the pans to form thin cheesecake bases. Bake for 15 minutes.
4. While the bases are baking, combine the remaining ingredients in a medium-sized bowl. Mix until smooth.
5. When the cheesecake bases have been baked, divide the remaining mixed ingredients evenly among the two mini pans.
6. Lower the oven temperature to 300°F.
7. Bake the cheesecakes until golden on the edges and the centers are almost set, about 35 to 40 minutes. Let cool before removing the rims.

Serving Suggestion: Serve topped with low-fat cream cheese.

Variation Tip: Add nuts for crunch.

Nutritional Information Per Serving:

Calories 454 | Carbohydrates 43.2g | Protein 7.5g | Fat 28g | Sodium 428.5mg| Fiber 3.4g

Mocha Cherry Pops

Prep Time: 5 minutes
Cook Time: 5 minutes
Serves: 6

Ingredients:

- 1 cup unsweetened vanilla almond milk
- 1 tablespoon instant espresso powder
- 3 packets Select Dark Chocolate Covered Cherry Shake
- 2 cups plain, low-fat Greek yogurt
- 1-2 packets zero-calorie sugar substitute
- 1 teaspoon vanilla extract

Preparation:

1. Microwave the milk in a microwave-safe mug or bowl for 45 seconds.
2. Immediately add the espresso powder, and stir until completely dissolved.
3. Once cooled, add the espresso milk and remaining ingredients to a blender or food processor. Blend until well combined and smooth.
4. Distribute the mixture evenly among six large popsicle molds, and freeze overnight.

Serving Suggestion: Serve chilled instantly after unmolding.

Variation Tip: You can use unsweetened plain almond milk or cashew milk.

Nutritional Information Per Serving:
Calories 21 | Carbohydrates 4g | Protein 2g | Fat 10g | Sodium 28mg| Fiber 0g

Gingerbread Trifle

Prep Time: 5 minutes
Cook Time: 10 minutes
Serves: 4

Ingredients:

- 2 sachets Essential Spiced Gingerbread
- 2 sachets Essential Creamy Vanilla Shake
- 12 ounces plain, low-fat Greek yogurt
- ½ cup pressurized whipped topping
- ¼ cup sugar-free salted caramel

Preparation:

1. Prepare the gingerbread as per the box instructions. Allow it to cool, and then cut it into small cubes.
2. In a mixing bowl, beat the vanilla shake mix with the Greek yogurt.
3. Evenly divide the yogurt mixture and cake cubes among four small trifle or parfait dishes.

Serving Suggestion: Serve the trifle topped with the whipped topping and drizzle with non-sugar syrup.

Variation Tip: Add fresh fruit if you like.

Nutritional Information Per Serving:

Calories 164 | Carbohydrates 24.7g | Protein 1.8g | Fat 6.3g | Sodium 218.8mg| Fiber 1.9g

Coconut Colada Shake

Prep Time: 2 minutes
Cook Time: 3 minutes
Serves: 1

Ingredients:
- 1 sachet Essential Creamy Vanilla Shake
- 6 ounces unsweetened, original coconut milk
- 6 ounces diet ginger ale
- 2 tablespoons unsweetened coconut, shredded
- ¼ teaspoon rum extract
- ½ cup ice

Preparation:

1. Set aside ½ tablespoon of the shredded coconut.
2. Combine all of the remaining ingredients in a blender, and blend until smooth and icy.
3. Divide the mixture among two piña colada glasses, and top with the remaining shredded coconut.

Serving Suggestion: Serve chilled.

Variation Tip: Add coconut shavings for a crunchy texture.

Nutritional Information Per Serving:
Calories 158.7 | Carbohydrates 23.1g | Protein 2.7g | Fat 6.6g | Sodium 39.1mg| Fiber 1.4g

Shrimp Cobb Salad

Prep Time: 10 minutes
Cook Time: 15 minutes
Serves: 1

Ingredients:

- 1 sachet Puffed Ranch Snacks
- 2 cups romaine lettuce
- 4 ounces shrimp, cooked and peeled
- ½ cup halved cherry or grape tomatoes
- 1 hard-boiled egg, sliced
- 1 slice turkey bacon, cooked and chopped
- ⅛ avocado, diced
- 1 tablespoon light ranch dressing

Preparation:

1. In a medium-sized bowl, combine the lettuce, shrimp, tomatoes, egg, turkey bacon, and avocado.
2. Top the salad with the dressing and the puffed snacks, and serve immediately.

Serving Suggestion: Serve the salad along with the crispy turkey bacon on the side.

Variation Tip: Add chopped nuts for extra crunch in the salad.

Nutritional Information Per Serving:

Calories 629.7 | Carbohydrates 12.9g | Protein 61g | Fat 36.1g | Sodium 1750.2mg| Fiber 3.2g

Chocolaty Peanut Butter Donuts

Prep Time: 10 minutes
Cook Time: 10 minutes
Serves: 4

Ingredients:

For the Donuts

- 2 sachets Essential Golden Chocolate Chip Pancakes
- 2 sachets Essential Decadent Double Chocolate Brownies
- 6 tablespoons liquid egg substitute
- ¼ cup unsweetened vanilla almond milk
- ½ teaspoon vanilla extract
- ½ teaspoon baking powder
- Cooking spray

For the Glaze

- ¼ cup powdered peanut butter
- 3-4 tablespoons unsweetened vanilla almond milk, to thin

Preparation:

1. Preheat the oven to 350°F.
2. Sift out the chocolate chips from the pancake mix and set them aside.
3. In a medium-sized bowl, combine the sifted pancake mix, brownie mix, egg substitute, milk, vanilla extract, and baking powder.
4. Divide the mixture evenly amongst four slots of a donut pan. Bake until the mixture is set, about 12 to 15 minutes. Let cool before glazing.
5. Meanwhile, prepare the peanut butter glaze. In a small shallow bowl, combine the powdered peanut butter and milk until smooth and slightly runny. Dip each donut into the glaze.

Serving Suggestion: Serve the glazed donuts topped with chocolate chips.

Variation Tip: Add butterscotch cream for taste.

Nutritional Information Per Serving:
Calories 360 | Carbohydrates 43g | Protein 3g | Fat 19g | Sodium 360mg| Fiber 1g

Cinnamon Bun Brownies

Prep Time: 10 minutes
Cook Time: 15 minutes
Serves: 4

Ingredients:

- 4 sachets Select Cinnamon Cream Cheese Swirl Cake
- ½ teaspoon cinnamon
- ½ teaspoon baking powder
- ⅔ cup unsweetened vanilla almond milk
- 2 tablespoons unsalted butter, melted
- 3 tablespoons liquid egg whites, divided
- 1⅓ ounces pecans, chopped
- Cooking spray
- ¼ cup light cream cheese, softened
- 1-2 packets zero-calorie sugar substitute
- ½ teaspoon vanilla extract

Preparation:

1. Preheat the oven to 350°F.
2. In a large bowl, combine the contents of the cake mix, cinnamon, and baking powder.
3. Add to the bowl the milk, butter, and 2 tablespoons of the liquid egg whites and stir until well combined. Fold in the pecans.
4. Pour the batter into a lightly-greased bread loaf pan.
5. In a small bowl, mix the cream cheese, sugar substitute, vanilla extract, and the remaining 1 tablespoon of egg white until well combined. Dollop the cream cheese mixture over the butter, and swirl with a knife.
6. Bake for 18 to 20 minutes until the batter is set and lightly browned.

Serving Suggestion: Serve warm.

Variation Tip: Add unsweetened low-fat chocolate chunks.

Nutritional Information Per Serving:

Calories 200 | Carbohydrates 27.5g | Protein 1.8g | Fat 9.7g | Sodium 79.8mg| Fiber 1.5g

Skinny Peppermint Mocha

Prep Time: 2 minutes
Cook Time: 3 minutes
Serves: 1

Ingredients:

- 1 sachet Essential Velvety Hot Chocolate
- 6 ounces freshly brewed coffee
- ¼ cup unsweetened almond milk
- ¼ teaspoon peppermint extract
- 2 tablespoons pressurized whipped topping
- A pinch of cinnamon

Preparation:

1. Combine the first three ingredients in a mug or coffee cup and stir until the hot chocolate mixture is fully dissolved.

Serving Suggestion: Serve topped with the whipped topping and sprinkle with cinnamon.

Variation Tip: Add unsweetened cocoa powder for an intense chocolaty flavor.

Nutritional Information Per Serving:
Calories 130 | Carbohydrates 17g | Protein 13g | Fat 1.5g | Sodium 150mg| Fiber 4g

Yogurt Donut with Cream Cheese

Prep Time: 10 minutes.
Cook Time: 15 minutes.
Serves: 2

Ingredients:

- 2 sachets Yogurt Berry Blast Smoothie
- 1/3 cup unsweetened almond milk
- 2 tablespoons liquid egg substitute
- ½ teaspoon baking powder
- Cooking spray
- 1 ounce cream cheese

Preparation:

1. Preheat oven to 350°F.
2. In a medium-sized bowl, combine the sachets of the smoothie mix, milk, egg substitute, and baking powder.
3. Divide the mixture among four lightly-greased slots of a donut pan.
4. Bake until the mixture is set, about 12 to 15 minutes.
5. Let cool slightly before serving with cream cheese.

Serving Suggestion: Serve topped with cream cheese.

Variation Tip: Top with chocolate chips.

Nutritional Information Per Serving:

Calories 363 | Carbohydrates 47g | Protein 2.7g | Fat 19g | Sodium 265mg| Fiber 0.9g

LEAN AND GREEN RECIPES

Salmon Burger with Cucumber Salad

Prep Time: 15 minutes
Cook Time: 15 minutes
Serves: 2

Ingredients:

For the Burger

- 1 egg, gently beaten
- 1½ tablespoons light mayo
- ½ teaspoon lemon juice
- 1 tablespoon onion, minced
- ¼ teaspoon dried parsley
- Dash of pepper
- 5 ounces can skinless and boneless pink salmon
- 1 packet multigrain crackers, crushed
- Cooking spray

For the Salad

- 5 ounces plain low-fat Greek yogurt
- 2 tablespoons apple cider vinegar
- 1 teaspoon fresh dill
- Dash of salt and pepper
- 3 cups cucumber, peeled and thinly sliced

Preparation:

1. Whisk the eggs with mayo, lemon juice, onion, parsley, and pepper. Gently fold in the salmon and crushed crackers.
2. Divide the mixture in half and shape it into patties.
3. Cook in a lightly greased pan over medium-high heat for around 5 minutes on each side.
4. Meanwhile, whisk the yogurt, vinegar, dill, salt, and pepper in a bowl.
5. Add the cucumber slices and stir to mix in. Chill until ready to serve.

Serving Suggestion: Serve the patties topped with the cucumber salad.
Variation Tip: You can also use dried dill instead of fresh.

Nutritional Information Per Serving:

Calories 350 | Fat 7.9g | Sodium 700mg | Carbohydrate 6g | Fiber 3.6g | Sugar 6g | Protein 18g

Vegetable Tofu Bowl with Eggs

Prep Time: 10 minutes
Cook Time: 20 minutes
Serves: 4

Ingredients:

- 2 pounds extra firm tofu
- ½ teaspoon each salt and pepper
- 2 teaspoons canola oil
- 1 cup small cauliflower florets
- 2 cups button mushrooms, cut in halves
- 1 medium red bell pepper, deseeded and diced
- 1 cup yellow summer squash, diced
- 1 cup tomatoes, diced
- 1½ tablespoons fresh ginger, finely minced
- 2 cloves garlic, finely minced
- 1½ tablespoons soy sauce
- 1 teaspoon sriracha
- 4 eggs
- ½ cup fresh cilantro, coarsely chopped
- 2 tablespoons low-fat parmesan cheese

Preparation:

1. Pat the tofu dry and cut it into cubes. Season with salt and pepper.
2. In a large wok, heat the oil and sear the tofu over medium-high heat until golden brown on all sides.
3. Add the cauliflower, mushrooms, peppers, squash, tomatoes, ginger, garlic, soy sauce, and sriracha along with two cups of water to the pot. Place the tofu on top and bring to a boil over high heat.
4. Once the mixture has started to boil, reduce the heat to medium-high and gently cook for 12 to 15 minutes.
5. Carefully crack the eggs in a pot of simmering water and cook for 5 minutes. Remove the eggs from the liquid.
6. Remove the vegetables and tofu (leaving the liquid in the wok) and place equally into four serving bowls and top with 1 egg each. Stir the cilantro into the liquid in the wok and pour over the bowls.

Serving Suggestion: Sprinkle each bowl with a sprinkling of parmesan cheese and serve hot.

Variation Tip: Add chopped veggies of your choice to the bowl.

Nutritional Information Per Serving:

Calories 357.2 | Carbohydrates 57.7g | Protein 20.4g | Fat 3g | Sodium 2521mg | Fiber 3.5g

Chicken Caesar Salad

Prep Time: 15 minutes
Cook Time: 30 minutes
Serves: 4

Ingredients:

For the Dressing

- 1 teaspoon fresh lemon juice
- 1 teaspoon Worcestershire sauce
- ½ teaspoon Dijon mustard
- 1 clove garlic, minced
- ¼ teaspoon salt
- ¼ teaspoon ground pepper
- 1 tablespoon parmesan cheese, grated
- 1½ tablespoons light mayo
- 3 teaspoons extra virgin olive oil

For the Salad

- Cooking spray
- 1 cup eggplant, chopped
- 1 cup zucchini, chopped
- 1 cup halved cherry tomatoes
- 6 cups romaine lettuce
- ¼ cup parmesan cheese, grated
- 1½ pounds grilled chicken breast, divided into chunks

Preparation:

1. Preheat the oven to 400°F.
2. Grease the baking sheet lightly with cooking spray and roast the eggplants and zucchini until tender, about 20 to 30 minutes.
3. Whisk together all the dressing ingredients in a small bowl.
4. Toss the roasted veggies, tomatoes, lettuce, dressing, and parmesan cheese together.

Serving Suggestion: Serve the salad topped with the grilled chicken chunks.

Variation Tip: Add chopped sweet bell pepper to the salad.

Nutritional Information Per Serving:
Calories 309 | Carbohydrates 8.2g | Protein 29g | Fat 17g | Sodium 476mg | Fiber 2.1g

Mediterranean Chicken and Vegetables

Prep Time: 15 minutes
Cook Time: 30 minutes
Serves: 4

Ingredients:

For the Chicken and Vegetables

- 4 raw boneless, skinless chicken breasts (8 ounces each)
- 3 Roma tomatoes, quartered
- 1 medium zucchini, cut into 8 wedges
- 1 yellow summer squash, cut into 8 wedges
- 1 large bell pepper, quartered
- 1 tablespoon canola oil
- ¼ teaspoon each salt and pepper
- 4 tablespoons reduced-fat feta

For the Dressing

- 2 garlic cloves, minced
- 1 tablespoon fresh oregano
- 2 tablespoons lemon juice
- 1 teaspoon olive oil

Preparation:

1. Preheat the oven to 375°F. Line a sheet pan with parchment paper and lightly grease with cooking oil or non-stick spray.
2. Place the chicken in a single layer on one side of the prepared pan.
3. Toss the veggies with oil, salt, and pepper. Transfer to the sheet pan separate from the chicken and in a single layer.
4. Place the pan in the oven and bake for about 15 minutes until the chicken reaches an internal temperature of 165°F.
5. Whisk the garlic, oregano, lemon juice, and olive oil in a small bowl for the dressing.

Serving Suggestion: To serve, place a chicken breast on a plate with some of the veggies and feta cheese. Drizzle the dressing on top and serve hot.

Variation Tip: You can use 1 teaspoon of dried oregano instead of fresh.

Nutritional Information Per Serving:

Calories 360 | Carbohydrates 35g | Protein 20g | Fat 16g | Sodium 880mg | Fiber 4g

Minestrone Soup

Prep Time: 10 minutes
Cook Time: 50 minutes
Serves: 4

Ingredients:

- 1¼ boneless skinless chicken thighs
- 4 cups chicken stock
- 1 teaspoon salt
- 1 cup celery, sliced
- 2 cups green cabbage, shredded
- 1 cup cooked yellow summer squash
- 1 cup halved cherry tomatoes
- 1 cup cauliflower florets
- ½ teaspoon ground black pepper
- 4 teaspoons low-fat parmesan cheese, grated

Preparation:

1. Combine the chicken and stock in a large pot and bring to the boil.
2. Once boiling, reduce the heat to low and simmer for 45 minutes.
3. Remove the chicken from the broth and set it aside to cool.
4. Add the veggies to the simmering broth and continue to simmer for 10 minutes.
5. Shred the chicken into bite-size pieces.
6. Add the chicken along with tomatoes, basil, and pepper to the pot.

Serving Suggestion: Serve the soup in bowls with a teaspoon of grated parmesan cheese per serving.

Variation Tip: You can add any of your favorite veggies to the soup.

Nutritional Information Per Serving:
Calories 50 | Carbohydrates 8g | Protein 2g | Fat 1g | Sodium 830mg| Fiber 2g

Shredded Beef Stew

Prep Time: 10 minutes
Cook Time: 35 minutes
Serves: 4

Ingredients:

- 1½ pound flank steak
- 2 cloves garlic, minced
- 1 teaspoon dried oregano
- 1 teaspoon ground cumin
- 1 teaspoon smoked paprika
- 1 bay leaf
- 1 (14 ½ ounces) can diced tomatoes
- ¼ teaspoon salt and pepper each
- 1 small bell pepper, deseeded and sliced
- 4 pitted green olives, halved
- 4 cups cauliflower rice

Preparation:

1. Add all the ingredients except for the peppers, olives, and cauliflower rice to a pressure or slow cooker. Secure the lid and adjust the timer to 30 minutes at high pressure (meat mode). When the cooking time is done, remove the beef.
2. Shred the beef with a fork and return it back to the pot with the bell pepper and olives and stir well.
3. Place the cauliflower rice in a steamer to steam for 5 minutes.

Serving Suggestion: Serve the beef stew over the cauliflower rice in a bowl.

Variation Tip: Adjust the seasonings as per your taste.

Nutritional Information Per Serving:

Calories 220.6 | Carbohydrates 6.6g | Protein 21.6g | Fat 10.4g | Sodium 770.2mg| Fiber 1g

Chicken Soy Chorizo Paella

Prep Time: 5 minutes
Cook Time: 35 minutes
Serves: 4

Ingredients:

- 4 teaspoons canola oil
- 2 ounces chorizo crumbles
- 1½ pounds boneless skinless chicken breast
- 2 cloves garlic, minced
- 1 scallion, trimmed and minced
- 4 cups cauliflower rice
- 1 cup tomatoes, diced
- 1 cup green beans, cut into ¼ inches pieces
- ¼ teaspoon salt and pepper each

Preparation:

1. In a skillet, add the oil and heat it over medium-high heat.
2. Add the chorizo until it has browned.
3. Add the chicken chunks and sauté well.
4. Add the garlic and scallions and stir for about 2 minutes. Add the cauliflower rice, tomatoes, and green beans to the skillet and cook for another 10 minutes.
5. Season with salt and pepper and simmer for an extra 5 minutes.

Serving Suggestion: Serve hot with your favorite beverage.

Variation Tip: Add a pinch of saffron for taste and color.

Nutritional Information per Serving:

Calories 87.5 | Carbohydrates 14.8g | Protein 6.1g | Fat 0.9g | Sodium 1577mg| Fiber 1.8g

Chicken Meatballs and Napa Cabbage in Ginger Broth

Prep Time: 10 minutes
Cook Time: 20 minutes
Serves: 4

Ingredients:

- 21 ounces lean minced chicken or turkey
- 1 large egg
- 1 teaspoon salt
- ½ teaspoon ground black pepper
- 2 tablespoons fresh ginger, minced
- 4 scallions, trimmed and minced
- 4 garlic cloves, minced
- 5 cups napa cabbage
- 2 cups chicken stock
- 4 green onions, trimmed and cut into 0.8-inch pieces

Preparation:

1. Combine the ground chicken or turkey, egg, salt, pepper, half of the ginger, and minced scallions into a bowl. Mix thoroughly.
2. Shape the meat mixture into meatballs of around 0.8 to 1 inches in size and set aside.
3. In a wok, combine the garlic, napa cabbage, chicken stock, and remaining ginger and bring to a boil.
4. Add the chicken or turkey meatballs and green onions to the wok, making sure that the broth covers them. Cook until the meatballs are done, and the cabbage is tender (about 5 minutes).

Serving Suggestion: Arrange in a bowl and garnish with chili oil and serve warm.

Variation Tip: These meatballs can also be made using lean beef mince.

Nutritional Information per Serving:

Calories 431 | Carbohydrates 7.1g | Protein 24.1g | Fat 34g | Sodium 990.6mg| Fiber 1.6g

Chicken Kohlrabi Noodles Soup

Prep Time: 10 minutes
Cook Time: 20 minutes
Serves: 4

Ingredients:

- 4 eggs
- 3 tablespoons reduced-sodium soy sauce
- 1¼ pound boneless skinless chicken breast
- 2½ pounds kohlrabi, thinly sliced, or 6 cups noodles
- 2 cups chicken broth
- 2 scallions, cut into ¼ inches rings
- ½ cup fresh basil
- ¼ teaspoon red pepper flakes
- 2 tablespoons toasted sesame seeds
- 1 teaspoon chili oil

Preparation:

1. Boil the eggs in water for about 6 minutes.
2. Peel the eggs and place them in a resealable bag. Add 2 tablespoons of the soy sauce to the bag, seal it, and gently shake to coat the eggs in the sauce. Marinate the eggs for an hour.
3. Marinate the chicken slices in 1 tablespoon of soy sauce for 1 hour.
4. Peel the kohlrabi and slice it to make long noodles. You can use a spiralizer for this step if you have one.
5. Boil the chicken broth, add the pepper flakes, kohlrabi noodles (or 6 cups regular noodles), and chicken. Simmer until the chicken is cooked and tender, about 10 minutes.
6. Stir in the scallion and basil.
7. Remove the eggs from the bag and cut them in half.

Serving Suggestion: Arrange equal amounts of broth along with the noodles and chicken into four soup bowls. Garnish with two half eggs, ½ tablespoon of sesame seeds, and ¼ teaspoon of chili oil per bowl. Serve hot.

Variation Tip: Zucchini or radish noodles may also be used in place of kohlrabi.

Nutritional Information Per Serving:
Calories 290| Carbohydrates 40g | Protein 14g | Fat 11g | Sodium 1770mg| Fiber 10g

Parmesan Meatballs with Collard Greens

Prep Time: 5 minutes
Cook Time: 58 minutes
Serves: 4

Ingredients:

- 4 cups water
- 12 cups collard greens, chopped
- 1½ cups chicken stock
- 1¼ pounds lean ground pork
- 2 eggs
- ½ teaspoon salt and pepper each
- 2 tablespoons low-fat parmesan cheese
- 1 tablespoon balsamic vinegar
- ¼ cup hemp, pumpkin, or sesame seeds

Preparation:

1. Boil the water in a saucepan and add the collard greens. Cover and cook until the collards are reduced to half their size, about 5 minutes.
2. Drain the water and add the stock to the greens. Simmer for 20 minutes on medium-low heat.
3. Make the meatballs by combining the pork, eggs, salt, and pepper. Shape the mix evenly into eight balls.
4. Add the meatballs to the collards and simmer for 20 more minutes.
5. Remove the meatballs and stir in the seeds, cheese, and balsamic vinegar to the green collard mix and simmer for another 5 minutes.

Serving Suggestion: Serve the meatballs on top of the braised collards.

Variation Tip: For a touch of spice, you can add chili flakes to the meatballs.

Nutritional Information Per Serving:

Calories 481| Carbohydrates 19g | Protein 26g | Fat 35g | Sodium 740mg| Fiber 9g

Spaghetti Squash Lasagna

Prep Time: 10 minutes
Cook Time: 50 minutes
Serves: 4

Ingredients:

- 1 medium spaghetti squash
- 4 teaspoon olive oil
- 1 teaspoon salt, divided
- 1 teaspoon pepper, divided
- 2 teaspoons garlic, minced
- 1 pound lean ground turkey
- 1 (14.5 ounces) canned tomatoes
- ½ teaspoon onion powder
- 1 teaspoon basil, divided
- 1 teaspoon oregano, divided
- ½ cup skim ricotta
- ½ cup cottage cheese
- 1 teaspoon crushed red pepper flakes
- 1 cup low-fat mozzarella, shredded

Preparation:

1. Preheat the oven to 400°F.
2. Prepare the spaghetti squash by cutting it in half and removing the seeds and pulp strands. Rub 1 teaspoon of olive oil into each half and season with salt and pepper.
3. Place each squash face down onto a lined baking dish and bake for about 50 minutes until tender and the inside is easily raked apart with a fork.
4. Meanwhile, in a saucepan, sauté the garlic in olive oil over medium heat until fragrant.
5. Add the turkey and season with salt and pepper, and cook until the meat is browned.
6. Add the tomatoes, onion powder, basil, and oregano. Cook for 5 minutes, then simmer until the sauce has thickened.
7. Combine the ricotta and cottage cheese in a bowl. Add the pepper flakes, oregano, basil, salt, and pepper, and mix lightly until well combined.
8. Carefully turn the spaghetti squash cut side up. Scrape the flesh of the spaghetti squash with a fork to make noodle-like strands and place them in a bowl. Add the cheese mix.
9. Evenly divide the noodle-cheese mix between the squash halves and spread the meat sauce over them. Top with the mozzarella cheese.
10. Turn the stove to broil, and place the squash back in. Cook the squash for an additional 2 minutes until the cheese is melted and browned.

Serving Suggestion: Serve while hot and bubbling.

Variation Tip: This recipe is a little spicy. For a milder taste, reduce the amount of crushed red pepper.

Nutritional Information Per Serving:

Calories 254.9 | Carbohydrates 5.5g | Protein 21.4g | Fat 15.9g | Sodium 306.1mg | Fiber 1g

Zucchini Lasagna

Prep Time: 5 minutes
Cook Time: 55 minutes
Serves: 4

Ingredients:

- 1 pound zucchini
- ¾ pound fresh tomatoes, sliced ⅛ inch thick
- 1¼ pound lean ground beef
- 3 ounces light cream cheese
- 1 teaspoon salt
- ½ teaspoon pepper
- 1 cup whole basil leaves
- 1 cup mozzarella, shredded

Preparation:

1. Preheat the oven to 425°F.
2. Slice the zucchini into ¼ inches lengthwise to make lasagna. Sprinkle with salt and allow to sit for 20 to 30 minutes.
3. In a pot, combine the beef with pepper, salt, and cream cheese.
4. Pat dry the zucchini slices and put a layer in a casserole dish topped with the ground beef. Top with the other layer of lasagna. Layer the casserole dish in the following sequence: lasagna sheet, ground beef, basil leaf and tomatoes, lasagna sheet.
5. Repeat the sequence until all the ingredients are used. Sprinkle mozzarella on top.
6. Bake the lasagna for about 30 minutes until golden.

Serving Suggestion: Cut into four portions and serve hot.

Variation Tip: For extra flavor, also add sliced bell pepper.

Nutritional Information Per Serving:
Calories 267 | Carbohydrates 9.8g | Protein 20g | Fat 17g | Sodium 818mg | Fiber 2.7g

Shepherd's Pie with Mashed Cauliflower

Prep Time: 10 minutes
Cook Time: 35 minutes
Serves: 4

Ingredients:

Mashed Cauliflower

- 5 cups riced cauliflower
- 3 large eggs
- ½ teaspoon salt
- 1 cup mozzarella, shredded
- ¼ cup parsley

Turkey Filling

- 1 pound turkey breast, cut into fine strips
- 1 cup mushrooms, sliced
- ½ teaspoon salt
- ½ cup sour cream
- 1 teaspoon paprika
- 1 teaspoon Worcestershire sauce

Preparation:

1. Bake the cauliflower rice on a flat, lined baking sheet for 30 minutes at 425°F until soft and golden brown.
2. Puree the baked cauliflower in a processor and mix with the eggs and salt.
3. Stir-fry the turkey and mushrooms in a non-stick pan with 2 tablespoons of water for about 5 to 7 minutes until the turkey is cooked. Add the sour cream, paprika, and Worcestershire sauce and mix well.
4. Place the turkey into a casserole dish. Spread the cauliflower mash evenly on top and sprinkle with the mozzarella.
5. Bake at 400°F for 15 minutes until browned. Garnish with parsley.

Serving Suggestion: Divide into four equal portions and serve hot.

Variation Tip: Add chopped chives or dill for a refreshing taste.

Nutritional Information Per Serving:
Calories 211 | Carbohydrates 11.6g | Protein 16.5g | Fat 10.6g | Sodium 581.4mg| Fiber 2.1g

Broccoli Cheddar Breakfast Bake

Prep Time: 10 minutes
Cook Time: 35 minutes
Serves: 4

Ingredients:

- 6 cups small broccoli florets
- 9 eggs
- 1 cup unsweetened almond milk
- ¼ teaspoon salt
- ¼ teaspoon ground pepper
- ¼ teaspoon cayenne pepper
- Cooking spray
- 4 ounces cheddar cheese, shredded

Preparation:

1. Preheat the oven to 375°F.
2. Place the broccoli with 3 tablespoons of water into a microwave-safe bowl. Microwave on high for 3 to 4 minutes until tender. Drain off the excess liquid.
3. Whisk the eggs with the milk and seasoning in a bowl.
4. Arrange the broccoli on the bottom of a lightly greased baking dish. Sprinkle the shredded cheese over the top and pour the egg mix on top.
5. Bake for 45 minutes until the center of the bake is set and a light brown crust has formed.

Serving Suggestion: Serve with crispy bacon on the side.

Variation Tip: Add mushrooms to enhance flavor.

Nutritional Information Per Serving:
Calories 138 | Carbohydrates 9g | Protein 11g | Fat 9g | Sodium 608mg| Fiber 1g

Blackened Shrimp Lettuce Wraps

Prep Time: 10 minutes
Cook Time: 10 minutes
Serves: 4

Ingredients:

- 2 pounds raw shrimp
- 1 tablespoon Old Bay Seasoning
- 4 teaspoons olive oil, divided
- 1 cup plain non-fat Greek yogurt
- 6 ounces avocado, peeled and pitted
- 2 tablespoons lime juice, divided
- 1½ cup tomatoes, diced
- ¼ cup green bell peppers, finely diced
- ¼ cup red onion, finely chopped
- ¼ cup fresh cilantro, chopped
- 1 medium jalapeno peppers, finely chopped
- 12 romaine lettuce leaves

Preparation:

1. Place the shrimp and seasoning in a re-sealable plastic bag. Shake the contents of the bag to distribute the seasoning evenly over the shrimp.
2. Heat two teaspoons of olive oil in a large skillet, and add half of the shrimp in a single layer. Cook for about 2 to 3 minutes per side until the shrimp are pink and cooked.
3. For the avocado mix: Combine the Greek yogurt, avocado, and lime juice in a blender. Blend until smooth.
4. For the salsa: Mix the tomatoes, bell pepper, onion, cilantro, jalapeno pepper, and lime juice in a medium bowl.

Serving Suggestion: Prepare the lettuce wraps by dividing the shrimp, avocado mix, and tomato salsa evenly among the lettuce leaves. Serve immediately.

Variation Tip: Add chopped bell pepper for color.

Nutritional Information Per Serving:
Calories 300| Carbohydrates 17g | Protein 18g | Fat 15g | Sodium 577mg| Fiber 2.5g

Cheeseburger Soup

Prep Time: 10 minutes
Cook Time: 35 minutes
Serves: 4

Ingredients:

- 1 pound lean ground beef
- ¼ cup onion, chopped
- ¾ cup celery, diced
- 1 (14.5 ounces) can diced tomatoes
- 3 cups low-sodium chicken broth
- 2 teaspoons Worcestershire sauce
- 1 teaspoon dried parsley
- ¼ teaspoon salt
- ¼ ground pepper
- 7 cups baby spinach
- 4 ounces reduced-fat cheddar cheese, shredded

Preparation:

1. In a large soup pot, cook the beef until browned.
2. Add the onion and celery, and sauté until tender. Remove from the heat and drain any excess liquid.
3. Stir in the tomatoes, broth, Worcestershire sauce, parsley, salt, and pepper. Cover and simmer on low heat for 20 minutes.
4. Add the spinach and cook until wilted (about 1 to 3 minutes).

Serving Suggestion: Serve the soup topped with cheese.

Variation Tip: Add your favorite veggies to the dish.

Nutritional Information Per Serving:

Calories 227.3 | Carbohydrates 16.1g | Protein 16.6g | Fat 10.7g | Sodium 675.4mg| Fiber 1.4g

Mexican Bell Pepper Casserole

Prep Time: 10 minutes
Cook Time: 50 minutes
Serves: 4

Ingredients:

- 3 large eggs
- 12 ounces low-fat plain Greek yogurt
- ½ cup onion, thinly sliced
- 1 clove garlic, minced
- 1 teaspoon olive oil
- ¼ teaspoon salt
- 1 teaspoon cumin
- ½ teaspoon coriander
- ½ teaspoon dry mustard
- ¼ teaspoon cayenne pepper
- 6 medium bell peppers, chopped
- 8 ounces reduced-fat cheese (cheddar, mozzarella), shredded

Preparation:

1. Preheat the oven to 375°F.
2. Beat the eggs and yogurt together.
3. Cook the onion and garlic with the spices in a saucepan until the onions are translucent. Add the bell peppers and continue cooking for about 8 to 10 minutes over low heat.
4. Spread the cooked pepper mix in a layer in a casserole dish and top with cheese. Repeat the layers until the ingredients run out. Pour the yogurt-egg mix over the top.
5. Cover with foil and bake for about 30 minutes. Then uncover and bake for another 15 minutes.

Serving Suggestion: Serve this yummy casserole topped with extra cheese if desired.

Variation Tip: This dish should only be cooked as instructed. Avoid using pre-made products as substitutes, such as onion sauces or other ingredients. You can use bell peppers of any color.

Nutritional Information Per Serving:
Calories 271.8 | Carbohydrates 20.1g | Protein 21.7g | Fat 11.6g | Sodium 302.5mg| Fiber 2.9g

Zucchini Pad Thai Noodles

Prep Time: 10 minutes
Cook Time: 25 minutes
Serves: 4

Ingredients:

For Peanut Sauce

- ½ cup powdered peanut butter
- 2 tablespoon lime juice
- 1 tablespoon lime zest
- 2 tablespoons low-sodium soy sauce
- 2 teaspoons fresh ginger, grated
- ½ teaspoon red pepper flakes
- 2-3 tablespoons water for thinning the sauce

For Zucchini Noodles

- 4 medium zucchinis
- 2 teaspoons olive oil
- Cooking spray
- 2 pounds raw shrimp, peeled and deveined
- 1 cup bell pepper, chopped
- ½ cup scallion, chopped
- 3 whole eggs
- ½ cup bean sprouts
- ½ cup fresh cilantro
- 2 tablespoons sesame seeds

Preparation:

1. Combine the peanut sauce ingredients in a small bowl and set aside.
2. Prepare the zucchini noodles using a spiralizer or by thinly slicing.
3. Heat the oil in a large pan over medium-high heat. Add the noodles and cook while occasionally stirring for 2 to 3 minutes. Drain the excess water from the noodles.
4. In a separate pan, sauté the shrimps until they become tender and pink (about 3 to 4 minutes).
5. Add the bell pepper and scallion and until tender.
6. Add the eggs and stir well until cooked.
7. Add the noodles back into the pan, add the peanut sauce, and cook for about 1 minute.

Serving Suggestion: Stir in the bean sprouts, cilantro, and sesame seeds and serve immediately.

Nutritional Information Per Serving:

Calories 170.9 | Carbohydrates 11.3g | Protein 20.8g | Fat 5.1g | Sodium 646mg| Fiber 2.6g

Maple Turkey Patties with Spaghetti Squash Hash Brown

Prep Time: 10 minutes
Cook Time: 50 minutes
Serves: 4

Ingredients:

For Spaghetti Squash Hash Browns

- 1 large spaghetti squash
- 1 cup scallions, chopped
- ½ teaspoon garlic powder
- 3 eggs
- ¼ teaspoon salt
- ½ teaspoon pepper
- 2 teaspoon olive oil
- 4 ounces low-fat cheddar cheese, shredded

For Maple Turkey Patties

- ½ teaspoon dried sage
- ½ teaspoon dried thyme
- ¼ teaspoon rosemary
- ¼ teaspoon nutmeg
- ¼ teaspoon salt
- ¼ teaspoon ground pepper
- 2 tablespoons sugar-free maple syrup
- 1 pound lean ground turkey
- 2 teaspoons olive oil

Preparation:

1. Preheat the oven to 400°F.
2. Cut the spaghetti squash in half lengthways. Scrape out the seeds and flesh. Brush the inside of the squash halves with olive oil and place the cut sides of the squash down on a foil-lined baking sheet.
3. Roast in the oven for around 30 to 40 minutes or until the flesh is fork-tender.
4. Scrape the flesh of the spaghetti squash with a fork to create noodles.
5. Combine the noodles, scallions, garlic powder, eggs, salt, pepper in a bowl to create the hash brown mixture.
6. Heat some oil in a frying pan, and then add the hash brown mixture (in a thin layer).
7. Cook until the underside is golden brown. Flip the hash brown over and cook until the other side is golden brown.
8. Using a spatula, cut the cooked hash brown up into four even pieces. Take the pieces out of the pan and set them aside on a paper towel on a plate.
9. Combine all the seasonings for the patties in a bowl.
10. Add in the syrup and the ground turkey and mix with your hands.

11. Form the turkey mixture into patties and cook in a skillet with olive oil until cooked.

Serving Suggestion: Top the hash browns with the shredded cheddar cheese and serve with the maple turkey patties.

Variation Tip: The hash brown can also be made from sweet potatoes rather than spaghetti squash.

Nutritional Information Per Serving:

Calories 330 | Carbohydrates 17g | Protein 40g | Fat 13g | Sodium 608mg| Fiber 2g

Egg Muffins with Kale, Tomatoes, and Goat's Cheese

Prep Time: 5 minutes
Cook Time: 25 minutes
Serves: 4

Ingredients:

- 9 eggs, gently beaten
- 1 cup liquid egg whites
- ¾ cup plain low-fat Greek yogurt
- 2 ounces crumbled goat's cheese
- ½ teaspoon salt
- 10 ounces kale, chopped
- 2 cups cherry tomatoes, chopped
- Cooking spray

Preparation:

1. Preheat the oven to 375°F.
2. Whisk the eggs, egg whites, Greek yogurt, goat's cheese, and salt in a large bowl until combined well.
3. Stir in the kale and cherry tomatoes.
4. Divide the mixture between 20 to 24 slots of a standard size greased muffin tin.
5. Bake for 20 to 25 minutes until the muffins are set in the middle. A knife inserted into the center of each one should come out clean.

Serving Suggestion: Serve warm with your morning coffee or to eat as a snack.

Variation Tip: Make these on the weekend and freeze them for the rest of the week. Simply pop one in the microwave for 1 minute and reheat.

Nutritional Information Per Serving:
Calories 290 | Carbohydrates 11g | Protein 29g | Fat 15g | Sodium 920mg| Fiber 3g

Spaghetti Squash Bolognese

Prep Time: 5 minutes
Cook Time: 30 minutes
Serves: 4

Ingredients:

- 1 medium spaghetti squash
- ½ teaspoon salt, divided
- ½ cup fresh basil
- 1¼ pounds lean ground beef
- 1 cup tomatoes, diced
- 2 scallions, trimmed and minced
- 1 cup water
- 1 tablespoon paprika
- ½ teaspoon each salt and pepper
- 2 tablespoons low-fat parmesan cheese

Preparation:

1. Preheat the oven to 400°F.
2. Prepare the spaghetti squash: Cut in half and remove the seeds and pulp strands. Rub 1 teaspoon of olive oil into each half and season with salt and pepper.
3. Place each squash face down into a lined baking dish and bake for about 50 minutes until tender and the insides fall apart easily.
4. Shred the flesh with a fork to make noodles and place them in a bowl.
5. Add salt to the noodles along with the basil leaves and mix well.
6. In a pan, combine the ground beef with the tomatoes, scallions, water, paprika, pepper, and salt.
7. Bring to a boil over medium heat, stirring constantly. Once the mixture has boiled, reduce the heat and simmer for 30 minutes.

Serving Suggestion: Top the spaghetti squash with the beef sauce and parmesan cheese.

Variation Tip: You can use chicken mince as a substitute for beef mince.

Nutritional Information Per Serving:

Calories 419.8 | Carbohydrates 17.3g | Protein 18.6g | Fat 28g | Sodium 424.7mg| Fiber 4.4g

Pepper Jack and Spinach Breakfast Burrito

Prep Time: 5 minutes
Cook Time: 20 minutes
Serves: 2

Ingredients:

For the Tortillas

- 2 eggs
- 4 egg whites
- 2 tablespoons whole flax seeds
- Cooking spray

For the filling

- 1 cup low-fat Pepper Jack cheese, shredded
- 2 cups baby spinach

For the Salsa

- 1 cup tomatoes, diced
- ½ cup bell pepper, diced
- 1 jalapeno pepper, diced
- 1 tablespoon red onion, chopped
- 1 clove garlic, minced
- 2 teaspoons balsamic vinegar
- ⅛ teaspoon salt
- ⅛ teaspoon pepper
- ¼ cup fresh cilantro, chopped

Preparation:

1. In a small bowl, whisk together all the tortilla ingredients.
2. Heat a lightly greased small skillet over medium-high heat. Pour half of the tortilla mix into the skillet and swirl it around to create an even tortilla.
3. Once the mix has hardened slightly, gently loosen it with the help of a spatula and carefully flip it over. Cook until the mixture is fully set. Repeat until all the tortilla mix has been cooked.
4. Lightly grease a pan and sauté the spinach until it has wilted, and then set it aside.
5. Combine all the salsa ingredients in a bowl.

Serving Suggestion: Place each tortilla on a large plate. Add some spinach, cheese, and salsa, roll into a burrito and then serve.

Variation Tip: To secure the burrito shape, wrap aluminum foil around the bottom half.

Nutritional Information Per Serving:

Calories 366 | Carbohydrates 30g | Protein 22g | Fat 22g | Sodium 666mg | Fiber 7g

Shrimp Fried Cauliflower Rice

Prep Time: 5 minutes
Cook Time: 30 minutes
Serves: 4

Ingredients:

- 2 tablespoons canola oil, divided
- 2 whole eggs
- 4 egg whites
- ¼ teaspoon each salt and pepper
- 2 scallions, minced
- 1½ pounds raw shrimp, peeled and deveined
- 1 cup bell pepper, diced
- 1 cup green beans, chopped
- 4 cups cauliflower rice
- 2 tablespoons soy sauce

Preparation:

1. In a wok, heat half of the oil and pour in the eggs, and scramble. Season with salt and pepper and set aside once done.
2. In a wok, add the remaining oil, scallions, and garlic and cook until fragrant.
3. Add the shrimps and cook for 2 minutes.
4. Add the bell pepper and green beans and cook for a minute. Once done, set aside.

Serving Suggestion: Fold the shrimp and vegetables into the scramble. Divide into four equal portions and enjoy.

Variation Tip: Use different colored peppers to add vibrancy.

Nutritional Information Per Serving:

Calories 239.2 | Carbohydrates 11.6g | Protein 27.7g | Fat 9.4g | Sodium 228.6mg| Fiber 4.8g

Buffalo Chicken Dip and Veggie Chips

Prep Time: 10 minutes
Cook Time: 45 minutes
Serves: 4

Ingredients:

For Veggie Chips

- 1 tablespoon olive oil
- 2 teaspoons lemon juice
- ½ teaspoon salt
- ½ teaspoon pepper
- ½ teaspoon rosemary
- 3 cups yellow squash, thinly sliced
- 3 cups zucchini, thinly sliced

For Buffalo Chicken dip

- 4 light spreadable cheese wedges
- 1½ cup plain Greek yogurt
- ¼ cup ranch dressing
- ¼ cup hot pepper sauce
- 1 (12 ½ ounces) can chicken breast chunks
- 1 cup moderate-fat Colby and Monterey Jack cheese, shredded
- Cooking spray

Preparation:

1. Preheat the oven to 400°F.
2. Whisk the olive oil, lemon juice, salt, pepper, and rosemary in a bowl.
3. Add the yellow squash and zucchini and gently coat with the mix.
4. On a large, lightly greased baking sheet, arrange the coated yellow squash and zucchini slices in a single layer. Bake for 20 to 30 minutes until crisp.
5. Mix all the dipping ingredients until smooth and transfer to a small, lightly greased baking dish. Bake for up to 15 to 20 minutes until light brown.

Serving Suggestion: Serve crispy chips with the dip.

Variation Tip: Add chopped dill to the dip for a fresh, citrus-like, earthy taste.

Nutritional Information Per Serving:

Calories 370 | Carbohydrates 22g | Protein 10g | Fat 28g | Sodium 680mg| Fiber 1g

Tuna Niçoise Salad

Prep Time: 5 minutes
Cook Time: 5 minutes
Serves: 4

Ingredients:

- 4 teaspoons extra virgin olive oil
- 3 tablespoons balsamic vinegar
- 2 garlic cloves, minced
- 6 cups mixed greens
- 1 cup halved grape tomatoes
- 2 cups steamed, tender string beans
- 6 hard-boiled eggs, sliced
- 2 (7 ounces each) cans of tuna

Preparation:

1. Whisk together the oil, vinegar, and garlic for the dressing.
2. Boil the eggs and then peel and slice them.
3. Prepare a bed of mixed greens.
4. Layer with the string beans, tomatoes, egg slices, and tuna, and drizzle with the dressing.

Serving Suggestion: Serve in bowls.

Variation Tip: You can purchase pre-cooked, hard-boiled, peeled eggs at the grocery store.

Nutritional Information Per Serving:

Calories 405| Carbohydrates 18.4g | Protein 39g | Fat 13.1g | Sodium 586mg| Fiber 6.2g

Crabmeat and Asparagus Frittata

Prep Time: 10 minutes
Cook Time: 20 minutes
Serves: 4

Ingredients:

- 2½ tablespoons extra virgin olive oil
- 2 pounds asparagus
- 1 teaspoon salt
- ½ teaspoon black pepper
- 2 teaspoons sweet paprika
- 1 pound crabmeat
- 1 tablespoon finely cut chives
- ¼ cup basil, chopped
- 4 cups liquid egg substitute

Preparation:

1. Preheat the oven to 375°F.
2. Remove the tough ends of the asparagus and cut them into bite-sized pieces.
3. In an oven-proof skillet, heat the olive oil and gently sweat the asparagus until tender, seasoning with salt, pepper, and paprika.
4. In a bowl, add the chives, basil, and crabmeat. Pour in the egg mixture and mix well.
5. Pour the mix onto the cooked asparagus. Cook over low to medium heat until the eggs start bubbling.
6. Place the skillet in the oven and bake for 15 to 20 minutes until the eggs are fully cooked.

Serving Suggestion: Serve with your choice of veggies on the side.

Variation Tip: Add chili flakes to the mixture for an extra kick.

Nutritional Information Per Serving:
Calories 169 | Carbohydrates 5g | Protein 16g | Fat 9g | Sodium 407mg| Fiber 1g

Savory Cilantro Salmon

Prep Time: 80 minutes
Cook Time: 35 minutes
Serves: 4

Ingredients:

- 4 cups fresh cilantro, divided
- 2 tablespoons fresh lemon juice
- 2 tablespoons hot red pepper sauce
- 1 teaspoon cumin
- ½ teaspoon salt, divided
- ½ cup water
- 4 (7 ounces each) raw salmon fillets
- 2 cups yellow bell pepper, sliced
- 2 cups red bell pepper, sliced
- 2 cups green bell pepper, sliced
- ½ teaspoon pepper
- Cooking spray

Preparation:

1. Preheat the oven to 400°F.
2. In a food processor, combine half the cilantro with the lemon juice, hot red pepper sauce, cumin, salt, and water. Purée until smooth.
3. Transfer the marinade into a large resealable bag. Add the salmon fillets to the bag and refrigerate for 1 hour, turning the bag occasionally.
4. Arrange the pepper slices in a single layer on a lightly greased baking dish and sprinkle with salt and pepper. Bake the slices for 20 minutes.
5. Drain the salmon. Top each fillet with the remaining chopped cilantro.
6. Place the salmon on top of the baked pepper slices and bake for 12 to 14 minutes until the fish flakes easily with a fork.

Serving Suggestion: Serve the salmon with the baked peppers on the side.

Variation Tip: You can chop the peppers into chunks instead of slices.

Nutritional Information Per Serving:

Calories 360 | Carbohydrates 15g | Protein 34g | Fat 11g | Sodium 910mg| Fiber 3g

Stuffed Eggplant with Shrimp and Cauliflower Rice

Prep Time: 10 minutes
Cook Time: 20 minutes
Serves: 4

Ingredients:

- 2 medium eggplants
- ½ teaspoon salt, divided
- 2½ tablespoons extra virgin olive oil
- 1¾ pound shrimp, peeled and deveined
- ⅛ teaspoon ground pepper
- 2 cups cauliflower rice
- 3 scallions, trimmed and minced
- ½ cup plain, low-fat Greek yogurt
- ½ cup parmesan cheese, grated

Preparation:

1. Preheat the oven to 450°F.
2. Cut each eggplant into eight 1½ to 3-inch rounds. Hollow out the pulp to make cups with a ½ inch thick bottom rim.
3. Chop up the scooped-out pulp and set it aside.
4. Season the eggplant cups with salt and pepper and roast them for about 18 minutes.
5. Prepare the stuffing by seasoning the shrimps and frying them in a skillet until pink on the outside.
6. In the same skillet, add olive oil and the chopped eggplant to the cauliflower rice and cook until tender.
7. Add the scallions and stir fry.
8. Combine the shrimps with the cauliflower rice mix and the yogurt.
9. Fill the roasted eggplants cups with the mixture and top with the parmesan cheese. Bake for 10 minutes until the cups are thoroughly cooked, and the cheese has melted.

Serving Suggestion: Serve the eggplant cups hot while the cheese is still bubbling.

Variation Tip: Sprinkle chives over the cooked cups for added freshness.

Nutritional Information Per Serving:

Calories 309 | Carbohydrates 9.6g | Protein 30.1g | Fat 16.9g | Sodium 605.4mg| Fiber 3.5g

Chilies Rellenos Omelet

Prep Time: 10 minutes
Cook Time: 10 minutes
Serves: 2

Ingredients:

- 2 poblano peppers
- 4 eggs, separated
- 2 tablespoons sour cream
- 1 small tomato
- ½ teaspoon chicken bouillon seasoning
- ½ teaspoon oregano
- ½ cup mushrooms, sliced
- ⅔ cup skim mozzarella, shredded and divided
- Cooking spray

Preparation:

1. Lightly coat the poblano peppers with cooking spray. Place on a lined baking sheet and broil until the skin appears dark (about 5 to 10 minutes). When done, remove, allow to cool, and then chop.
2. In a small bowl, combine the egg yolks and sour cream.
3. In another bowl, beat the egg whites until fluffy and soft peaks start to form.
4. Gently fold the yolks into the egg white mixture until thoroughly combined.
5. For the sauce: Peel and chop the tomato and combine with the bouillon seasoning and oregano until smooth.
6. For the omelet: Pour half of the egg mixture into a lightly greased skillet. Cook until the bottom is set and golden and the top is fluffy. Top it with cheese, peppers, and mushrooms. Fold it and cook until the cheese has melted.

Serving Suggestion: Serve the omelet straight from the skillet with tomato sauce.

Variation Tip: Add extra spices or herbs according to your taste.

Nutritional Information Per Serving:

Calories 535 | Carbohydrates 2g | Protein 26g | Fat 46g | Sodium 567mg| Fiber 0g

Huevos Rancheros

Prep Time: 10 minutes
Cook Time: 15 minutes
serves: 1

Ingredients:

- 2 tablespoons olive oil, divided
- ½ cup jalapeno, sliced
- ½ cup tomato, diced
- ½ cup bell pepper, diced
- ¼ teaspoon garlic, minced
- 1 medium onion
- 2 eggs
- ⅛ teaspoon salt
- ¼ teaspoon pepper
- 1½ ounces avocado, sliced
- ½ cup fresh cilantro
- 1 lime, cut into wedges
- 2 ready-made tortillas

Preparation:

1. Heat 1 tablespoon of oil in a large pan. Add the onions with a pinch of salt, and cook until translucent, around 3 to 4 minutes. Add the garlic and cook for a minute more.
2. Add the tomatoes to the pan and cook until mixed.
3. Heat the remaining oil in a large frying pan over medium-high heat. Crack in the eggs, and then reduce the heat to low. Cook slowly until the whites are completely firm.
4. To assemble, spread the tomato and onion sauce onto the tortillas, add the tomatoes and jalapeños and sprinkle with cheese. Top with some avocado, a squeeze of lime juice, and a fried egg, then scatter with coriander. Serve with lime wedges on the side.

Serving Suggestion: Serve the eggs topped with sautéed vegetables, avocado, and fresh cilantro.

Variation Tip: Add 1 teaspoon of hot pepper sauce for spiciness.

Nutritional Information Per Serving:

Calories 327.3 | Carbohydrates 37.3g | Protein 26.3g | Fat 8.2g | Sodium 1391.1mg| Fiber 7.7g

Bell Pepper Eggs

Prep Time: 5 minutes
Cook Time: 10 minutes
Serves: 1

Ingredients:

- 1 medium bell pepper
- Cooking spray
- 3 eggs
- 1/8 teaspoon salt
- 1/8 teaspoon pepper

Preparation:

1. Cut the bell pepper into 3-inch rings and deseed.
2. Heat a skillet over high heat and lightly coat with cooking spray. Cook the pepper rings on both sides (about 1 minute).
3. Carefully pour the contents of 1 egg into a pepper ring. Repeat with all the rings and eggs.
4. Sprinkle salt and pepper on top and cover. Cook for 3 to 5 minutes until the eggs are fully cooked and set.

Serving Suggestion: Serve with sautéed veggies like zucchini, bell pepper, and asparagus.

Variation Tip: Add diced tomatoes to the eggs before pouring them into the pepper rings for an extra yummy taste.

Nutritional Information Per Serving:

Calories 121.5 | Carbohydrates 4 g | Protein 8.6g | Fat 7.9g | Sodium 151mg| Fiber 1g

Cumin Tacos De Bistec

Prep Time: 10 minutes
Cook Time: 20 minutes
Serves: 4

Ingredients:

- 2 pounds top round roast, minced
- 2 tablespoons lime juice
- ½ tablespoon cumin
- ¼ teaspoon each salt and pepper
- 16 taco shells
- 8 radishes, sliced thin
- 1 cup fresh cilantro, chopped

Preparation:

1. Combine the beef with lime, cumin, salt, and pepper.
2. Heat a lightly greased non-stick pan on high and add the beef mixture.
3. Brown the beef, stirring occasionally, until cooked through.
4. Prepare the tortillas by heating them on a skillet.

Serving Suggestion: Serve the beef in taco shells with sliced radishes and cilantro.

Variation Tip: Add chopped cabbage for extra crunch.

Nutritional Information Per Serving:

Calories 121.5 | Carbohydrates 4g | Protein 8.6g | Fat 7.9g | Sodium 157mg| Fiber 1g

Beef Stew over Mashed Cauliflower

Prep Time: 10 minutes
Cook Time: 6 hours
Serves: 4

Ingredients:

- ½ teaspoon salt
- ¼ teaspoon pepper
- ½ teaspoon onion powder
- 1½ pounds boneless chuck roast, fat trimmed
- 8 ounces baby bella mushrooms, sliced
- 3 cups low-sodium chicken broth, divided
- 2 teaspoons Dijon mustard
- 2 teaspoons balsamic vinegar
- 1 tablespoon sugar-free maple syrup
- 1 teaspoon thyme
- 2 cloves garlic, minced, divided
- 1 (16 ounces) bag frozen cauliflower florets

Preparation:

1. Rub the salt, pepper, and onion powder on the chuck roast and place it in a slow cooker. Add the mushrooms.
2. Whisk the chicken broth with the mustard, vinegar, syrup, thyme, and garlic. Pour the mix over the chuck roast.
3. Cook the chuck roast for 6 hours on high.
4. Cook the frozen cauliflower and mash it into a puree. Season to taste.

Serving Suggestion: Serve the beef stew on top of the mashed cauliflower and enjoy.

Variation Tip: For extra depth of flavor, the chuck roast on low for 8 hours.

Nutritional Information Per Serving:

Calories 495 | Carbohydrates 38g | Protein 52g | Fat 15g | Sodium 670mg| Fiber 5g

Cincinnati Chili

Prep Time: 10 minutes
Cook Time: 35 minutes
Serves: 4

Ingredients:

- 1 pound lean ground beef
- ½ cup leeks, chopped
- 3 cups tomatoes, diced
- ½ cup water
- 1 garlic clove, minced
- 1 teaspoon unsweetened cocoa powder
- 1 teaspoon Worcestershire sauce
- 1 teaspoon chili powder
- 1 teaspoon cinnamon
- 1 teaspoon ground cumin
- 1 bay leaf
- ¼ teaspoon ground allspice
- ½ teaspoon salt
- 1 spaghetti squash
- 1 cup cheddar cheese, shredded

Preparation:

1. Preheat the oven to 400°F.
2. In a large pot, cook the beef and leeks until brown and tender.
3. Add the tomatoes, water, garlic, cocoa powder, and Worcestershire sauce along with the bay leaf, herbs, and spices. Mix well and cook until thickened.
4. Reduce the sauce to a simmer, cover, and cook for about 20 minutes.
5. Prepare the spaghetti squash: Cut in half and remove the seeds and pulp strands. Rub 1 teaspoon of olive oil into each half and season with salt and pepper. Place each squash half face down onto a lined baking dish and bake for about 50 minutes until tender, and the flesh can fall apart easily. Shred the flesh with a fork and place it in a bowl.
6. Remove the bay leaf from the chili and mix in the spaghetti squash.

Serving Suggestion: Serve the chili topped with cheese.

Variation Tip: Add chopped scallion for garnishing.

Nutritional Information Per Serving:
Calories 114.8 | Carbohydrates 7.8g | Protein 12.4g | Fat 4.5g | Sodium 501mg| Fiber 2.1g

Cloud Bread

Prep Time: 10 minutes
Cook Time: 35 minutes
Serves: 4

Ingredients:

For Bread Base

- 3 eggs, separated
- 3 tablespoons full-fat cream cheese
- 1 sachet calorie-free sweetener
- ¼ teaspoon cream of tartar
- Cooking spray

For Garlic Bread Seasoning

- ½ tablespoon unsalted butter, melted
- ¼ teaspoon garlic powder
- ¼ teaspoon Italian seasoning
- ¼ teaspoon salt

Preparation:

1. Preheat the oven to 300°F.
2. In a bowl, mix the egg yolks, cream cheese, and sugar substitute until well combined.
3. In a large bowl, combine the egg whites and cream of tartar and beat on high until stiff peaks form.
4. Fold the egg yolk mixture into the egg whites until well combined.
5. Scoop the mixture into even rounds on a baking sheet, bake for 20 minutes, and remove from the oven.
6. Brush the tops with the butter, sprinkle with the garlic bread seasoning and bake for another five minutes until the tops are golden brown.

Serving Suggestion: Serve the bread warm with your favorite beverage.

Variation Tip: Add 1 teaspoon of olive oil, half a teaspoon of rosemary, and a quarter teaspoon of salt to the bread base to make focaccia bread.

Nutritional Information Per Serving:

Calories 35.1 | Carbohydrates 0.5g | Protein 2.2g | Fat 2.6g | Sodium 42.3mg| Fiber 0g

Cauliflower Tortillas

Prep Time: 10 minutes
Cook Time: 10 minutes
Serves: 2

Ingredients:

- 2 cups riced cauliflower
- ½ cup liquid egg substitute
- ⅔ cup mozzarella cheese, shredded
- ½ teaspoon salt

Preparation:

1. Preheat the oven to 425°F.
2. Combine all the ingredients in a bowl and mix well.
3. Divide the mix evenly into two tortilla shapes on a baking sheet lined with parchment paper. Place another parchment paper on top and lightly press down.
4. Bake for 30 minutes, turning over after 15 minutes to make sure both sides are cooked. The edges may turn a golden brown.

Serving Suggestion: Serve the tortillas with your favorite beef sauce.

Variation Tip: Add 1 teaspoon of sodium-free seasoning for taste and avoid using salt.

Nutritional Information Per Serving:
Calories 42 | Carbohydrates 5g | Protein 3g | Fat 1g | Sodium 120mg| Fiber 2g

4-Ingredients Skinny Queso

Prep Time: 5 minutes
Cook Time: 10 minutes
Serves: 4

Ingredients:

- ½ cup unsweetened almond milk
- 1½ cups sharp cheddar cheese, shredded
- ¾ cup low-fat plain Greek yogurt
- ½ cup tomatoes and green chilies, diced
- 1 pound mini sweet peppers

Preparation:

1. In a saucepan, heat the almond milk to a simmer.
2. Remove the saucepan from the heat and add the cheese, stirring until it has completely melted.
3. Add the diced tomatoes, chilies, and yogurt and mix until all the ingredients are well combined.

Serving Suggestion: Serve with halved mini sweet peppers for dipping.

Variation Tip: You can also use baby carrots and celery sticks for dipping.

Nutritional Information Per Serving:

Calories 190 | Carbohydrates 12g | Protein 15g | Fat 10g | Sodium 420mg| Fiber 3g

Pepper Nachos

Prep Time: 5 minutes
Cook Time: 15 minutes
Serves: 4

Ingredients:

- ¼ cup jalapeño pepper, diced
- Cooking spray
- 1 (12 ounces) can chicken breast, drained
- 6 ounces avocado, mashed
- ½ cup plain Greek yogurt
- 2 cups low-fat cheddar cheese, shredded and divided
- 1 teaspoon chili powder
- 24 mini bell peppers
- ¼ cup scallions, chopped

Preparation:

1. Sauté the diced jalapeno in a lightly greased pan until tender.
2. Mix the jalapeno with the chicken, avocado, yogurt, cheese, and chili powder in a bowl.
3. Arrange the mini bell peppers in a single layer in a casserole dish. Add the chicken mixture, sprinkle with the remaining cheese and broil until melted.

Serving Suggestion: Garnish with chopped scallions and serve with salsa.

Variation Tip: Add cauliflower tortilla chips for extra crunch.

Nutritional Information Per Serving:
Calories 153 | Carbohydrates 5g | Protein 25g | Fat 8g | Sodium 315mg| Fiber 1g

Chicken with Tomato Braised Cauliflower

Prep Time: 10 minutes
Cook Time: 30 minutes
Serves: 4

Ingredients:

- 3 scallions, trimmed and chopped
- 4 cloves garlic, minced
- ¼ teaspoon crushed red pepper flakes
- ¼ teaspoon dried oregano
- 1½ cups canned diced tomatoes
- 4 ½ cups cauliflower florets
- ¼ cup water
- ½ teaspoon salt and pepper each
- 1 cup fresh basil, gently torn
- 1½ pounds boneless skinless chicken breast
- 1½ tablespoons olive oil

Preparation:

1. Preheat the oven to 450°F.
2. In a saucepan, combine the scallions, garlic, pepper flakes, oregano, tomatoes, and cauliflower florets with the water.
3. Bring everything to a boil, season with salt and pepper, and cover. Simmer for 10 minutes until the cauliflower is tender.
4. Toss the chicken with olive oil and roast in the oven for 20 minutes. Once done, cool the chicken for about 10 minutes.

Serving Suggestion: Slice the chicken and serve on a bed of tomato braised cauliflower.
Variation Tip: Add chopped bell pepper for extra crunch.

Nutritional Information Per Serving:

Calories 143.2 | Carbohydrates 10.1g | Protein 17g | Fat 4g | Sodium 113mg| Fiber 4.6g

Vegetable and Turkey Pizza

Prep Time: 10 minutes
Cook Time: 35 minutes
Serves: 4

Ingredients:

- 5 ounces ground turkey
- 1 egg
- 1 cup cauliflower
- 1 cup spinach
- 4 ounces mozzarella cheese
- ½ cup grapes tomatoes, thinly sliced
- 1 teaspoon garlic, minced
- ¼ teaspoon Italian seasoning

Preparation:

1. Preheat the oven to 450°F.
2. Steam the cauliflower and mash when tender.
3. Sauté the ground turkey with some of the Italian seasoning.
4. For the pizza base: Combine the egg, half a cup of the cheese, the mashed cauliflower, garlic, and Italian seasoning in a bowl and mix well.
5. Spread the pizza base mixture evenly onto a non-stick pizza pan, bake for 20 minutes, and remove from the oven.
6. Top the cooked pizza base with the tomatoes, spinach, ground turkey, and mozzarella.
7. Broil the pizza until the cheese has melted and the turkey has browned (about 10 minutes).

Serving Suggestion: Cut into standard pizza slices and serve.

Variation Tip: Add olives and basil for taste.

Nutritional Information Per Serving:

Calories 240.7 | Carbohydrates 38.2g | Protein 10.6g | Fat 6.0g | Sodium 501.2mg| Fiber 6.7g

Turkey Chili

Prep Time: 10 minutes
Cook Time: 35 minutes
Serves: 4

Ingredients:

- 1½ pounds lean ground turkey
- 2 tablespoons onion, diced
- 2 garlic cloves, minced
- 1 medium red bell pepper, diced
- 1 medium green bell pepper, diced
- 1 jalapeno pepper, diced
- 2 teaspoons olive oil
- 1 (28 ounces) can diced tomatoes
- 1 cup water
- 1½ teaspoons ground cumin
- 2 teaspoons chili powder
- ¼ teaspoon crushed red pepper flakes
- ¼ teaspoon salt

Toppings (Per Serving)

- 2 tablespoons scallions, chopped
- 1½ ounces avocado, diced
- 2 tablespoons low-fat Greek yogurt
- 3 tablespoons low-fat cheddar cheese, shredded

Preparation:

1. In a large soup pot, sauté the onions, garlic, and peppers in oil for five minutes until tender.
2. Add the turkey and cook until brown.
3. Pour in the tomatoes, water, cumin, chili powder, pepper flakes, and salt and mix until well blended. Cover and simmer on low for about 20 minutes.

Serving Suggestion: Serve in bowls with the toppings.

Variation Tip: You can use chicken mince instead of turkey.

Nutritional Information Per Serving:

Calories 224 | Carbohydrates 19.68g | Protein 19.75g | Fat 7.75g | Sodium 1000mg| Fiber 6.1g

Chicken Cacciatore

Prep Time: 10 minutes
Cook Time: 6-8 hours
Serves: 4

Ingredients:

- 4 (7 ounces each) raw boneless skinless chicken thighs
- 2 cloves garlic, minced
- 2 scallions, minced
- 1 small bell pepper, deseeded
- 1 cup button mushroom, halved
- 1 can diced tomatoes
- 1 bay leaf
- 1 large zucchini, spiralized
- ¼ cup fresh basil, chopped
- ¼ teaspoon each salt and pepper

Preparation:

1. Combine the chicken, garlic, bell peppers, mushrooms, tomatoes, bay leaf, salt, and pepper in a slow cooker. Set on low for 6 to 8 hours.
2. Once done, stir in the zucchini noodles and basil. Mix thoroughly to combine.

Serving Suggestion: Serve in bowls in the required amount.

Variation Tip: Add chopped bell pepper for color.

Nutritional Information Per Serving:

Calories 221 | Carbohydrates 7.9g | Protein 23.4g | Fat 11.3g | Sodium 668mg| Fiber 3.1g

Baked Pork Chops with Sautéed Chard and Mushrooms

Prep Time: 5 minutes
Cook Time: 1 hour
Serves: 4

Ingredients:

- 1½ pounds boneless pork chops
- ½ teaspoon salt, divided
- ¼ teaspoon pepper, divided
- 1 teaspoon dried thyme
- Cooking spray
- ¼ cup low-sodium chicken broth
- 8 ounces baby bella mushrooms, sliced
- 4 cloves garlic, minced
- ⅛ teaspoon red pepper flakes
- 20 ounces Swiss chard, washed and chopped
- ¼ cup parmesan cheese, grated

Preparation:

1. Preheat the oven to 450°F.
2. Season the pork chops with salt, pepper, and thyme.
3. Lightly grease a large skillet and heat the pork chops until light brown.
4. Pour the chicken broth into a pot and heat, then sauté the mushrooms with garlic and red pepper flakes until tender.
5. Arrange the chard in a large casserole dish and season with salt and pepper. Add the mushroom mixture followed by the pork chops. Top with cheese.
6. Bake for 18 to 20 minutes until done.

Serving Suggestion: Serve the chops with chards and mushrooms.

Variation Tip: Add chopped bell pepper for crunch.

Nutritional Information Per Serving:

Calories 260 | Carbohydrates 9g | Protein 31g | Fat 11g | Sodium 322mg| Fiber 2g

Ropa Vieja

Prep Time: 10 minutes
Cook Time: 35 minutes
Serves: 4

Ingredients:

- 1½ pound flank steak
- 2 cloves garlic, minced
- 1 teaspoon oregano
- 1 teaspoon cumin
- 1 teaspoon paprika powder
- 1 bay leaf
- 1 (14½ ounces) can diced tomatoes
- ¼ teaspoon each salt and pepper
- 1 small bell pepper
- 4 pitted green olives, halved
- 4 cups riced cauliflower

Preparation:

1. Add all of the ingredients except the bell pepper, olives, and cauliflower rice to a slow cooker. Cover the lid and cook for about 6 hours on slow until the meat is tender.
2. Shred the beef and add back to the slow cooker along with the bell peppers and olives. Cook on low for another hour.
3. Cook the cauliflower rice.

Serving Suggestion: Serve the shredded beef stew over the cooked cauliflower rice.

Nutritional Information Per Serving:
Calories 340 | Carbohydrates 9.3g | Protein 34.2g | Fat 18g | Sodium 1223mg| Fiber 1.3g

Lemony Garlicky Chicken with Asparagus

Prep Time: 10 minutes
Cook Time: 35 minutes
Serves: 4

Ingredients:

- 1¾ pounds bone-in, skinless chicken thighs
- 1 small lemon, juiced
- 2 cloves garlic, minced
- 2 tablespoons fresh oregano
- ¼ teaspoon each salt and pepper
- 2 pounds asparagus, trimmed

Preparation:

1. Preheat the oven to 350°F.
2. Put the chicken in a bowl with the lemon juice, salt, pepper, garlic, and oregano and toss well to combine. Transfer to a casserole dish or baking sheet.
3. Roast the chicken in the oven for about 40 minutes.
4. Steam the asparagus and sprinkle with salt and pepper.

Serving Suggestion: Serve the asparagus with the roasted chicken thighs.

Variation Tip: For a bit of spice, add crushed pepper flakes.

Nutritional Information Per Serving:

Calories 120 | Carbohydrates 4g | Protein 16g | Fat 3.5g | Sodium 920mg| Fiber 1g

Chicken Pho

Prep Time: 10 minutes
Cook Time: 30 minutes
Serves: 4

Ingredients:

- 1 pound boneless, skinless chicken breast
- ½ teaspoon salt
- ½ teaspoon ground black pepper
- 3 cups fat-free chicken broth
- 3 cups water
- 3 lettuce stems, spiralized into noodles
- 1 cup bean sprouts
- ½ medium onion, thinly sliced
- 2 tablespoons sesame oil
- ½ cup cilantro
- ½ cup basil leaves
- 2 fresh red-hot chili peppers, deseeded
- 1 spring onion, trimmed and chopped

Preparation:

1. Place the chicken in a large pot and add salt and pepper. Add the water and bring to a boil.
2. Once boiling, reduce the heat to a simmer for about 15 to 20 minutes until the chicken is cooked.
3. Remove the cooked chicken from the water and shred.
4. Add the chicken broth to the pot of water. Add noodles and boil.
5. Place a serving of noodles at the bottom of a bowl and top with chicken, bean sprouts, and onion.
6. Add the broth and sesame oil. Garnish with basil, chili, and spring onion.

Serving Suggestion: Add crispy bacon for some crunch.

Variation Tip: For extra spiciness, add chili oil on top of each serving.

Nutritional Information Per Serving:

Calories 246 | Carbohydrates 27g | Protein 24.1g | Fat 4.2g | Sodium 623.3mg| Fiber 2.5g

Arroz Con Pollo

Prep Time: 10 minutes
Cook Time: 25 minutes
Serves: 4

Ingredients:

- 1¾ pounds boneless skinless chicken breast
- ¼ teaspoon salt and pepper
- 2 cloves garlic, minced
- 1 scallion, minced
- 4 cups cauliflower rice
- 1½ cups halved cherry tomatoes
- 40 pitted green olives
- ½ cup green beans

Preparation:

1. Preheat the oven to 350°F.
2. Season the chicken with salt and pepper and place on a greased baking dish. Bake for 20 minutes.
3. In a large saucepan, combine all the remaining ingredients and simmer on low heat for 8 to 10 minutes.
4. Slice the cooked chicken breast.

Serving Suggestion: Serve the chicken with the veggie-cauliflower rice mix.

Variation Tip: For a more traditional look, cut the chicken into bite-size chunks and cook with the cauliflower rice.

Nutritional Information Per Serving:
Calories 556 | Carbohydrates 35g | Protein 32g | Fat 33g | Sodium 145mg| Fiber 3g

Tropical Chicken Medley

Prep Time: 10 minutes
Cook Time: 50 minutes
Serves: 4

Ingredients:

- 2 pounds boneless, skinless chicken breast, cut into strips
- 3 cups broccoli, chopped
- 1½ cups red bell pepper, chopped
- 1½ cups yellow bell pepper, chopped
- ½ cup light, lime vinaigrette dressing
- 2 teaspoons onion powder
- 1 teaspoon garlic and herb seasoning blend
- ½ ounce pine nuts
- Cooking spray

Preparation:

1. Coat the chicken breast strips with the lime dressing.
2. Sprinkle the seasoning blend and onion powder onto the chicken strips. Marinate for 30 minutes.
3. Sauté the pepper and broccoli in a pot with little oil until al dente. Add the marinated chicken to the pan and cook thoroughly.
4. Meanwhile, toast the pine nuts in a small pan until brown.

Serving Suggestion: Serve the chicken with vegetables and topped with toasted nuts.

Variation Tip: Include other veggies of your choice.

Nutritional Information Per Serving:
Calories 370 | Carbohydrates 16g | Protein 55g | Fat 12g | Sodium 577mg | Fiber 3g

Shrimp Scampi

Prep Time: 5 minutes
Cook Time: 35 minutes
Serves: 4

Ingredients:

- 1 small-sized spaghetti squash
- 1½ tablespoons olive oil
- 1 clove garlic, minced
- 1¾ pound cooked shrimp
- 1 cup cherry tomatoes, halved
- ½ teaspoon red pepper flakes
- 1 teaspoon lemon juice
- 1 tablespoon dried parsley
- ½ teaspoon onion powder
- ¼ teaspoon salt
- ¼ teaspoon ground pepper
- ¼ cup parmesan cheese, grated

Preparation:

1. Preheat the oven to 400°F.
2. Prepare the spaghetti squash: Cut the squash in half and remove the seeds and pulp strands. Rub 1 teaspoon of olive oil into each half and season with salt and pepper. Place each squash face down onto a lined baking dish and bake for about 50 minutes until tender and the flesh falls apart easily. Shred the flesh with a fork and transfer to a bowl.
3. Measure out 5 cups of squash flesh.
4. Heat a large skillet over medium-high heat, add olive oil, and swirl to coat the pan. Sauté the garlic until fragrant (about 1 minute).
5. Add the shrimps, tomatoes, pepper flakes, lemon juice, parsley, onion powder, salt, and pepper. Cook for 3 to 4 minutes.
6. Add the spaghetti squash flesh and cook until heated through.

Serving Suggestion: Serve the scampi topped with parmesan cheese.

Variation Tip: Add mozzarella and broil until the cheese is golden and melted.

Nutritional Information Per Serving:

Calories 239 | Carbohydrates 5g | Protein 23g | Fat 12g | Sodium 1357mg| Fiber 0.2g

Crabmeat Burger with Salad

Prep Time: 5 minutes
Cook Time: 35 minutes
Serves: 2

Ingredients:

- 1 (10 ounces) can crabmeat
- 1 egg
- 1½ tablespoons mayo
- ½ tablespoon lemon juice
- 1 tablespoon onion, minced
- ¼ teaspoon each salt and pepper
- Cooking spray
- ¼ teaspoon dried parsley
- 1 packet multigrain crackers, crushed
- 1 packet green salad

Preparation:

1. Whisk the eggs with the mayo, lemon juice, onion, parsley, and pepper. Gently fold in crabmeat and crushed crackers.
2. Divide the mixture in half and shape it into two patties.
3. Cook in a lightly greased pan over medium-high heat for about 5 minutes on each side.
4. Meanwhile, whisk the yogurt, vinegar, dill, salt, and pepper in a salad bowl.
5. Add the green salad to the yogurt mixture and stir to mix in. Chill until ready to serve.

Serving Suggestion: Serve the patties topped with the green salad.

Variation Tip: Add cheese chunks to the salads.

Nutritional Information Per Serving:
Calories 195 | Carbohydrates 17g | Protein 10g | Fat 10g | Sodium 370mg| Fiber 3g

LEAN AND GREEN MEAL PLAN 5 & 1

This beginner's plan includes five fuelings and one balanced Lean and Green meal each day. What follows is an example of the types of fuelings and meals that can be eaten daily. You can swap any of these with the relevant recipes in this book.

Week 1

DAY 1	FUELING HACKS	• Buffalo cauliflower wings • Mashed potato and grilled cheese waffle • Red velvet cream pies • Greek yogurt sticks • Sweet potato and goat's cheese quiche
	LEAN & GREEN MEAL	• Chicken soy chorizo paella
DAY 2	FUELING HACKS	• Pecan and sweet potato muffin • Chocolate berry parfait • Peanut butter energy bites • Honey chicken nuggets • Oatmeal breakfast cookies
	LEAN & GREEN MEAL	• Beef/shredded beef stew
DAY 3	FUELING HACKS	• Taco salad • Crunchy caramel parfait • Yogurt berry bagel with cream cheese • Tropical smoothie bowl • Honey chicken nuggets
	LEAN & GREEN MEAL	• Minestrone soup
DAY 4	FUELING HACKS	• Pumpkin chocolate cheesecake • Mocha cherry pops • Shrimp Cobb salad • Chocolate coconut cream pie • Skinny peppermint mocha
	LEAN & GREEN MEAL	• Mediterranean chicken and vegetables
DAY 5	FUELING HACKS	• Yogurt donut with cream cheese • Skinny peppermint mocha • Taco salad • Pumpkin chocolate cheesecake • Lemon bites
	LEAN & GREEN MEAL	• Chicken Caesar salad
DAY 6	FUELING HACKS	• Coconut colada shake

			• Shrimp Cobb salad
			• Lemon bites
			• Cheesy savory waffles
			• Oatmeal breakfast cookies
		LEAN & GREEN MEAL	• Vegetable tofu bowl with eggs
DAY 7		FUELING HACKS	• Honey chicken nuggets
			• Guacamole with zesty chips
			• Chocolate berry parfait
			• Pecan and sweet potato muffin
			• Gingerbread trifle
		LEAN & GREEN MEAL	• Salmon burger with cucumber salad

Week 2

DAY 1	FUELING HACKS	• Buffalo cauliflower wings • Mashed potato and grilled cheese waffle • Red velvet cream pies • Greek yogurt sticks • Sweet potato and goat's cheese quiche
	LEAN & GREEN MEAL	• Chicken meatballs and napa cabbage in ginger broth
DAY 2	FUELING HACKS	• Pecan and sweet potato muffin • Chocolate berry parfait • Peanut butter energy bites • Honey chicken nuggets • Oatmeal breakfast cookies
	LEAN & GREEN MEAL	• Chicken kohlrabi noodles soup
DAY 3	FUELING HACKS	• Honey chicken nuggets • Guacamole with zesty chips • Chocolate berry parfait • Pecan and sweet potato muffin • Gingerbread trifle
	LEAN & GREEN MEAL	• Parmesan meatballs and collard greens
DAY 4	FUELING HACKS	• Coconut colada shake • Shrimp Cobb salad • Lemon bites • Cheesy savory waffles • Oatmeal breakfast cookies
	LEAN & GREEN MEAL	• Spaghetti squash lasagna

DAY 5	FUELING HACKS	• Chocolaty peanut butter donut • Skinny peppermint mocha • Taco salad • Pumpkin chocolate cheesecake • Lemon bites
	LEAN & GREEN MEAL	• Shepherd's pie with mashed cauliflower
DAY 6	FUELING HACKS	• Taco salad • Crunchy caramel parfait • Yogurt berry bagel with cream cheese • Tropical smoothie bowl • Honey chicken nuggets
	LEAN & GREEN MEAL	• Cheeseburger soup
DAY 7	FUELING HACKS	• Pecan and sweet potato muffin • Chocolate berry parfait • Peanut butter energy bites • Honey chicken nuggets • Oatmeal breakfast cookies
	LEAN & GREEN MEAL	• Broccoli cheddar breakfast bake

Week 3

DAY 1	FUELING HACKS	• Yogurt donut with cream cheese • Skinny peppermint mocha • Shrimp Cobb salad • Coconut colada shake • Peanut butter energy bites
	LEAN & GREEN MEAL	• Blackened shrimp lettuce wraps
DAY 2	FUELING HACKS	• Honey chicken nuggets • Oatmeal breakfast cookies • Taco salad • Pumpkin chocolate cheesecake • Lemon bites
	LEAN & GREEN MEAL	• Cheeseburger soup
DAY 3	FUELING HACKS	• Skinny peppermint mocha • Taco salad • Pumpkin chocolate cheesecake • Pecan and sweet potato muffin • Gingerbread trifle
	LEAN & GREEN MEAL	• Mexican bell pepper casserole

DAY 4	FUELING HACKS	• Pecan and sweet potato muffin • Chocolate berry parfait • Honey chicken nuggets • Guacamole with zesty chips • Pecan and sweet potato muffin
	LEAN & GREEN MEAL	• Zucchini Pad Thai noodles
DAY 5	FUELING HACKS	• Buffalo cauliflower wings • Mashed potato and grilled cheese waffle • Chocolaty peanut butter donut • Skinny peppermint mocha • Shrimp Cobb salad
	LEAN & GREEN MEAL	• Spaghetti squash Bolognese
DAY 6	FUELING HACKS	• Pecan and sweet potato muffin • Chocolate berry parfait • Peanut butter energy bites • Honey chicken nuggets • Oatmeal breakfast cookies
	LEAN & GREEN MEAL	• Pepper Jack and spinach burrito
DAY 7	FUELING HACKS	• Red velvet cream pies • Greek yogurt sticks • Sweet potato and goat's cheese quiche • Guacamole with zesty chips • Pecan and sweet potato muffin
	LEAN & GREEN MEAL	• Shrimp fried cauliflower rice

Week 4

DAY 1	FUELING HACKS	• Yogurt donut with cream cheese • Skinny peppermint mocha • Honey chicken nuggets • Oatmeal breakfast cookies • Taco salad
	LEAN & GREEN MEAL	• Tuna Niçoise salad
DAY 2	FUELING HACKS	• Shrimp Cobb salad • Coconut colada shake • Peanut butter energy bites • Pumpkin chocolate cheesecake • Lemon bites

	LEAN & GREEN MEAL	• Huevos rancheros
DAY 3	FUELING HACKS	• Skinny peppermint mocha • Taco salad • Pumpkin chocolate cheesecake • Pecan and sweet potato muffin • Chocolate berry parfait
	LEAN & GREEN MEAL	• Cumin tacos de bistec
DAY 4	FUELING HACKS	• Pumpkin chocolate cheesecake • Pecan and sweet potato muffin • Gingerbread trifle • Honey chicken nuggets • Guacamole with zesty chips
	LEAN & GREEN MEAL	• Chicken with tomato braised cauliflower
DAY 5	FUELING HACKS	• Skinny peppermint mocha • Shrimp Cobb salad • Pecan and sweet potato muffin • Chocolate berry parfait • Peanut butter energy bites
	LEAN & GREEN MEAL	• Vegetable and turkey pizza
DAY 6	FUELING HACKS	• Buffalo cauliflower wings • Mashed potato and grilled cheese waffle • Chocolaty peanut butter donut • Honey chicken nuggets • Oatmeal breakfast cookies
	LEAN & GREEN MEAL	• Chicken cacciatore
DAY 7	FUELING HACKS	• Sweet potato and goat's cheese quiche • Guacamole with zesty chips • Pecan and sweet potato muffin • Shrimp Cobb salad • Coconut colada shake
	LEAN & GREEN MEAL	• Ropa vieja

LEAN AND GREEN MEAL PLAN 4 & 2 & 1

This plan is designed for those who need more calories and flexibility in their food choices. This plan intended to provide four fuelings, two Lean and Green meals, and one snack per day. For variation, you can swap these fuelings and meals with other recipes included in this book.

Week 1

DAY 1	**FUELING HACKS**	• Yogurt donut with cream cheese • Skinny peppermint mocha • Honey chicken nuggets • Oatmeal breakfast cookies
	SNACK	• Shrimp Cobb salad
	LEAN & GREEN MEAL	• Tuna Niçoise salad • Crabmeat burger with salad
DAY 2	**FUELING HACKS**	• Shrimp Cobb salad • Coconut colada shake • Peanut butter energy bites • Pumpkin chocolate cheesecake
	SNACK	• Cobb salad
	LEAN & GREEN MEAL	• Huevos rancheros • Tropical chicken medley
DAY 3	**FUELING HACKS**	• Skinny peppermint mocha • Taco salad • Pumpkin chocolate cheesecake • Pecan and sweet potato muffin
	SNACK	• Honey chicken nuggets
	LEAN & GREEN MEAL	• Cumin tacos de bistec • Arroz con pollo
DAY 4	**FUELING HACKS**	• Pumpkin chocolate cheesecake • Pecan and sweet potato muffin • Gingerbread trifle • Honey chicken nuggets
	SNACK	• 12 cashews
	LEAN & GREEN MEAL	• Chicken with tomato braised cauliflower • Pepper nachos
DAY 5	**FUELING HACKS**	• Skinny peppermint mocha

		• Shrimp Cobb salad • Pecan and sweet potato muffin • Chocolate berry parfait
	SNACK	• Mixed nuts with tea
	LEAN & GREEN MEAL	• Vegetable and turkey pizza • Skinny queso
DAY 6	FUELING HACKS	• Buffalo cauliflower wings • Mashed potato and grilled cheese waffle • Chocolaty peanut butter donut • Honey chicken nuggets
	SNACK	• 10 almonds and 3 celery stalks
	LEAN & GREEN MEAL	• Chicken cacciatore • Shrimp scampi
DAY 7	FUELING HACKS	• Sweet potato and goat's cheese quiche • Guacamole with zesty chips • Pecan and sweet potato muffin • Shrimp Cobb salad
	SNACK	• ½ cup whole wheat pasta with grated parmesan
	LEAN & GREEN MEAL	• Ropa vieja • Cumin tacos de bistec

Week 2

DAY 1	FUELING HACKS	• Yogurt donut with cream cheese • Skinny peppermint mocha • Honey chicken nuggets • Oatmeal breakfast cookies
	SNACK	• 20 peanuts
	LEAN & GREEN MEAL	• Salmon burger with cucumber salad • Vegetable tofu bowl with eggs
DAY 2	FUELING HACKS	• Shrimp Cobb salad • Coconut colada shake • Peanut butter energy bites • Pumpkin chocolate cheesecake
	SNACK	• 12 cashews
	LEAN & GREEN MEAL	• Chicken Caesar salad • Minestrone soup

DAY 3	**FUELING HACKS**	• Skinny peppermint mocha • Taco salad • Pumpkin chocolate cheesecake • Pecan and sweet potato muffin	
	SNACK	• Celery sticks with natural cheese	
	LEAN & GREEN MEAL	• Mediterranean chicken and vegetables • Chicken soy chorizo paella	
DAY 4	**FUELING HACKS**	• Pumpkin chocolate cheesecake • Pecan and sweet potato muffin • Gingerbread trifle • Honey chicken nuggets	
	SNACK	• ½ sliced apple with three walnuts	
	LEAN & GREEN MEAL	• Chicken with tomato braised cauliflower • Beef/shredded beef stew	
DAY 5	**FUELING HACKS**	• Skinny peppermint mocha • Shrimp Cobb salad • Pecan and sweet potato muffin • Peanut butter energy bites	
	SNACK	• String cheese	
	LEAN & GREEN MEAL	• Chicken meatball with napa cabbage broth • Zucchini noodles	
DAY 6	**FUELING HACKS**	• Buffalo cauliflower wings • Mashed potato and grilled cheese waffle • Chocolaty peanut butter donut • Honey chicken nuggets	
	SNACK	• 12 cashews	
	LEAN & GREEN MEAL	• Parmesan meatballs and collard greens • Spaghetti squash lasagna	
DAY 7	**FUELING HACKS**	• Sweet potato and goat's cheese quiche • Guacamole with zesty chips • Pecan and sweet potato muffin • Shrimp Cobb salad	
	SNACK	• Turkey jerky	
	LEAN & GREEN MEAL	• Shepherd's pie with mashed cauliflower • Broccoli cheddar breakfast bake	

Week 3

DAY 1	**FUELING HACKS**		• Yogurt donut with cream cheese • Skinny peppermint mocha • Honey chicken nuggets • Oatmeal breakfast cookies
	SNACK		• Feta cheese with tomatoes
	LEAN & GREEN MEAL		• Cheeseburger soup • Bell pepper casserole
DAY 2	**FUELING HACKS**		• Shrimp Cobb salad • Coconut colada shake • Peanut butter energy bites • Pumpkin chocolate cheesecake
	SNACK		• Shrimp Cobb salad
	LEAN & GREEN MEAL		• Pad Thai noodles • Turkey patties with hash brown
DAY 3	**FUELING HACKS**		• Skinny peppermint mocha • Taco salad • Pecan and sweet potato muffin • Chocolate berry parfait
	SNACK		• Avocado slices
	LEAN & GREEN MEAL		• Egg muffins with kale • Spaghetti squash Bolognese
DAY 4	**FUELING HACKS**		• Pumpkin chocolate cheesecake • Pecan and sweet potato muffin • Gingerbread trifle • Guacamole with zesty chips
	SNACK		• Kale chips
	LEAN & GREEN MEAL		• Pepper Jack and spinach burrito • Buffalo chicken dip and veggie chips
DAY 5	**FUELING HACKS**		• Skinny peppermint mocha • Shrimp Cobb salad • Pecan and sweet potato muffin • Chocolate berry parfait
	SNACK		• Tuna Niçoise salad
	LEAN & GREEN MEAL		• Cumin tacos de bistec • Cincinnati chill

DAY 6	FUELING HACKS	• Buffalo cauliflower wings • Mashed potato and grilled cheese waffle • Chocolaty peanut butter donut • Oatmeal breakfast cookies
	SNACK	• 12 almonds
	LEAN & GREEN MEAL	• Bell pepper eggs • Huevos rancheros
DAY 7	FUELING HACKS	• Sweet potato and goat's cheese quiche • Guacamole with zesty chips • Pecan and sweet potato muffin • Shrimp Cobb salad
	SNACK	• 3 walnuts with cheese sticks
	LEAN & GREEN MEAL	• Pepper nachos • Turkey chili

Week 4

DAY 1	FUELING HACKS	• Yogurt donut with cream cheese • Skinny peppermint mocha • Honey chicken nuggets • Taco salad
	SNACK	• Blackberries
	LEAN & GREEN MEAL	• Crabmeat and asparagus frittata • Pepper nachos
DAY 2	FUELING HACKS	• Shrimp Cobb salad • Coconut colada shake • Pumpkin chocolate cheesecake • Lemon bites
	SNACK	• 3 walnuts with cheese sticks
	LEAN & GREEN MEAL	• Vegetable and turkey pizza • Cincinnati chili
DAY 3	FUELING HACKS	• Skinny peppermint mocha • Pumpkin chocolate cheesecake • Pecan and sweet potato muffin • Chocolate berry parfait
	SNACK	• Celery and cheese
	LEAN & GREEN MEAL	• Tropical chicken medley • Shrimp scampi

DAY 4	**FUELING HACKS**	• Pumpkin chocolate cheesecake • Pecan and sweet potato muffin • Honey chicken nuggets • Guacamole with zesty chips
	SNACK	• Cherry tomatoes with olive oil
	LEAN & GREEN MEAL	• Crabmeat burger with salad • Tuna Niçoise salad
DAY 5	**FUELING HACKS**	• Skinny peppermint mocha • Shrimp Cobb salad • Pecan and sweet potato muffin • Peanut butter energy bites
	SNACK	• Mixed nuts
	LEAN & GREEN MEAL	• Shrimp fried cauliflower rice • Egg muffins with kale
DAY 6	**FUELING HACKS**	• Buffalo cauliflower wings • Mashed potato and grilled cheese waffle • Honey chicken nuggets • Oatmeal breakfast cookies
	SNACK	• Sliced bell pepper with mustard dip
	LEAN & GREEN MEAL	• Spaghetti squash Bolognese • Tuna Niçoise salad
DAY 7	**FUELING HACKS**	• Sweet potato and goat's cheese quiche • Guacamole with zesty chips • Pecan and sweet potato muffin • Coconut colada shake
	SNACK	• Sliced bell pepper with your favorite dip
	LEAN & GREEN MEAL	• Chilies rellenos omelet • Beef/shredded beef stew

CONCLUSION

The Lean and Green diet promotes weight loss and other health benefits via low-calorie prepackaged foods, homemade low-carb meals, and personalized coaching. It is helpful for people wanting to shed some pounds as well as those looking to control their blood pressure.

Although the beginner's 5 & 1 Plan is relatively restrictive in order to stimulate weight loss, the 3 & 3 maintenance phase allows for a greater variety of food and fewer snacks, making it easier to maintain your weight loss in the long term.

Any restrictive diet comes with its pros and cons, and the Lean and Green diet is no exception. Some may find that the prepackaged foods are expensive, that sticking to a low-carb diet can become repetitive, and that restricting certain foods might not satisfy all their nutritional needs. Additionally, extended calorie or carb restriction can result in nutrient deficiencies and potential health problems.

However, while the program initially encourages quick weight and fat loss, it also aims to provide a foundation for better health in the long run. The recipes of the maintenance plan promote healthy eating habits (restricting processed carbs and sugar) and regular, scheduled eating. The recipes are designed to boost digestion and slow energy release and provide sufficient daily nutritional intake. If followed carefully, the Lean and Green diet will support your weight loss journey, now and in the future.

As with any weight-loss program, please consult with a physician or nutritionist to ensure that it's the right diet for you.

I wish you the best of luck on your weight loss journey!

Copyright © 2021
All Right Reserved.

Under no circumstances may any part of this publication be reproduced, distributed, or transmitted in any form or by any means, including photocopying, recording, or other electronic or mechanical methods, or by any information storage and retrieval system without the prior written permission of the copyright holder.

The information in this book is accurate and complete. However, the author and the publisher do not warrant the accuracy of the information, text, and graphics contained within the book due to the rapidly changing nature of science, research, known and unknown facts, and the internet. The author and the publisher do not hold any responsibility for errors, omissions or contrary interpretation of the subject matter herein. This book is presented solely for motivational and informational purposes only.

CONCLUSION

The Lean and Green diet promotes weight loss and other health benefits via low-calorie prepackaged foods, homemade low-carb meals, and personalized coaching. It is helpful for people wanting to shed some pounds as well as those looking to control their blood pressure.

Although the beginner's 5 & 1 Plan is relatively restrictive in order to stimulate weight loss, the 3 & 3 maintenance phase allows for a greater variety of food and fewer snacks, making it easier to maintain your weight loss in the long term.

Any restrictive diet comes with its pros and cons, and the Lean and Green diet is no exception. Some may find that the prepackaged foods are expensive, that sticking to a low-carb diet can become repetitive, and that restricting certain foods might not satisfy all their nutritional needs. Additionally, extended calorie or carb restriction can result in nutrient deficiencies and potential health problems.

However, while the program initially encourages quick weight and fat loss, it also aims to provide a foundation for better health in the long run. The recipes of the maintenance plan promote healthy eating habits (restricting processed carbs and sugar) and regular, scheduled eating. The recipes are designed to boost digestion and slow energy release and provide sufficient daily nutritional intake. If followed carefully, the Lean and Green diet will support your weight loss journey, now and in the future.

As with any weight-loss program, please consult with a physician or nutritionist to ensure that it's the right diet for you.

I wish you the best of luck on your weight loss journey!

Copyright © 2021 All Right Reserved.

Under no circumstances may any part of this publication be reproduced, distributed, or transmitted in any form or by any means, including photocopying, recording, or other electronic or mechanical methods, or by any information storage and retrieval system without the prior written permission of the copyright holder.

The information in this book is accurate and complete. However, the author and the publisher do not warrant the accuracy of the information, text, and graphics contained within the book due to the rapidly changing nature of science, research, known and unknown facts, and the internet. The author and the publisher do not hold any responsibility for errors, omissions or contrary interpretation of the subject matter herein. This book is presented solely for motivational and informational purposes only.